Grieving

the Loss of a

Loved One

DAILY MEDITATIONS

Lorene Hanley Duquin

OUR SUNDAY VISITOR PUBLISHING DIVISION
OUR SUNDAY VISITOR, INC.
HUNTINGTON, INDIANA 46750

Copyright © 2012 by Lorene Hanley Duquin.
Published 2012.

17 16 15 14 13 12   1 2 3 4 5 6 7 8 9

ISBN: 978-1-61278-566-0 (Inventory No. T1264)
eISBN: 978-1-61278-292-8
LCCN: 2012950284

Cover design: Amanda Falk
Cover art: Shutterstock
Interior design: Dianne Nelson

PRINTED IN THE UNITED STATES OF AMERICA

CONTENTS

Introduction 6

1. The Journey Through Grief 8
2. The Initial Shock 10
3. Telling the Story 12
4. Asking Why 14
5. The Way We Grieve 16
6. Suppressing Grief 18
7. Why Do I Feel Like This? 20
8. Time 22
9. The Gift of Tears 24
10. The Problem of Sleep 26
11. Feeling Crushed 28
12. Feeling Crazy 30
13. Making Decisions 32
14. Helping Ourselves 34
15. The Mystery of Death 36
16. Where Is God? 38
17. Who Am I? 40
18. Memories 42
19. Sadness 44
20. Anger 46
21. Blame 48
22. Regrets 50
23. Forgiveness 52
24. Fear 54
25. Loneliness 56

26. Secondary Losses 58
27. Advice From Other People 60
28. When People Avoid Us. 62
29. The People Who Help 64
30. Doing Little Things. 66
31. Visiting the Cemetery. 68
32. Temptations. 70
33. Dealing With Doubts. 72
34. Giving Up Control 74
35. Lighting Candles 76
36. Where Did They Go?. 78
37. The Communion of Saints. 80
38. Praying for Our Loved Ones 82
39. Problems With Prayer. 84
40. Trying to Understand. 86
41. Letting Go. 88
42. The Resurrection of the Body 90
43. The Gift of Laughter 92
44. Grief Surges. 94
45. Grieving Together. 96
46. Dreading Special Days 98
47. Looking at a Bigger Picture 100
48. Gratitude 102
49. Hope 104
50. Healing 106
51. The New Normal 108
52. In Our Hearts. 110

Acknowledgments 112

Introduction

WHEN MY EDITOR at Our Sunday Visitor, Bert Ghezzi, left a message on my answering machine asking if I would be interested in writing a book of meditations for people who are grieving, my first impulse was to say no. I was still in the throes of my own grief over the death of my mother. My mother had been ill for a long time. She still lived in the old family homestead. I had quit my job in order to spend more time with her and watched her gradual decline. I thought I was prepared for her death, but I was not.

How could I do a book of meditations on grief when I was grieving?

I decided to pray about it.

I was no newcomer when it came to grief. I had undergone bereavement training when I was working as a pastoral associate and had started grief-support ministries in several parishes. I had given talks on grieving. I had written articles about bereavement and a book for Our Sunday Visitor entitled *Grieving with the Help of Your Catholic Faith*.

But even with all that bereavement information in my head, my mother's death was more difficult than I had ever imagined. It struck me in the heart. I felt as if something deep inside me had been ripped out. I had difficulty concentrating. I felt sick to my stomach most of the time. Thoughts of my mother consumed me. And I faced the additional pain of having to clean out and sell the family homestead.

How could I do a book of meditations on grief when I was grieving?

So I kept praying.

Then my editor asked me to write a few meditations to see how this book might be structured. I sat down and asked God to help me. The meditation on tears seemed to unfold in my mind. I prayed some more, and the next meditation that came to me was dealing with doubts.

It wasn't long before I realized that writing a book of meditations is not like writing a how-to book. I discovered that this book of meditations would be rooted in prayer, in the inspirations of the Holy Spirit, in my own experiences of grieving, and in my desire to help others who were grieving.

So I agreed to write the book. I quickly realized that this little book of meditations was helping me grieve the loss of my mother. I sincerely hope it will help you grieve the loss of your loved one.

Grief is a very individual process. Every person grieves differently. You may find that some of the meditations describe exactly what you are experiencing. Other meditations may not relate to your particular situation at all. Don't feel as if you have to read this book cover to cover. You can pick and choose the meditations that are most helpful. There may be some that you will want to read often and some that you will read only once. It's okay.

If there's one message that I would like to present throughout this book it is that you should never feel bound by anything that someone else tells you to do when you're grieving. You will know in the depths of your own being what is right. Follow your interior guide. You will eventually come to realize that what you feel inside is the Holy Spirit – leading you, inspiring you, comforting you, and healing you.

My final prayer is that the Lord will bless you and give you peace as you journey through your grief.

1. The Journey Through Grief

Grief is like a long valley, a winding valley where any bend may reveal a totally new landscape.
— C. S. Lewis

GRIEF IS THE PAINFUL JOURNEY that we embark upon when someone we love dies. It is not unlike the recovery period after a serious surgery, when our bodies need time to heal and our muscles need time to regenerate.

When we lose a loved one, a significant part of our lives is torn away. In trying to describe the severity of the loss, Madeleine L'Engle wrote: "The death of a beloved is an amputation." But unlike a physical amputation, where we lose a limb, the death of a loved one is an emotional amputation, where we lose a person that we loved deeply.

Grief is the process by which we allow ourselves to come to grips with our loss. It is a journey that will be different for each of us, depending on our personalities and our relationship with the person who died.

Some of us will travel through the classic stages of grief: shock, denial, anger, sadness, and gradual acceptance. Others will jump back and forth from one stage to another. Some of us may skip some of the stages entirely. There is no right or wrong way to move through grief.

Grief is not an illness or an abnormality. It is a natural process. We grieve deeply because we loved deeply.

Grief is also a holy process. In his Sermon on the Mount, Jesus tells us: "Blessed are they who

8

mourn, for they will be comforted" (Mt 5:4). Jesus is telling us that we are blessed, not because the loss of a loved one was a blessing, but because we will be comforted in our loss. Jesus doesn't tell us how we will be comforted. He only promises that he will help us through this difficult time. Is our faith strong enough to believe in that promise?

PRAYER: *Lord, be my comfort and my strength as I journey through grief. You know the depths of pain in my heart. You know how lost and weak I feel. Guide me through each stage of this journey. Strengthen my faith and my trust in you. Never let me be separated from you. Amen.*

❖❖❖❖❖

A good reflection for beginning our journey through grief comes from the prophet Isaiah, who assures us that God will be with us, no matter what we encounter on our journey:

> *When you pass through waters, I will be with you;*
>   *through rivers, you shall not be swept away.*
> *When you walk through fire, you shall not be burned,*
>   *nor will flames consume you.*
> *For I, the LORD, am your God,*
>   *the Holy One of Israel, your savior. (Is 43:2-3)*

❖❖❖❖❖

2. THE INITIAL SHOCK

The shock of her death froze something in me.
— VLADIMIR NABOKOV

WHETHER THE DEATH was unexpected or whether we had been anticipating it for a long time, there is always a sense of disbelief when it happens. We feel numb — almost as if we have been frozen in time. We may feel as if we are in a trance — going through the motions of what we have to do and say — but not feeling anything.

Shock in the early stages of our grief is God's way of protecting us from the harsh reality of death for a while. We know that our loved one is gone, but the full impact has not gripped us yet. We keep saying, "I can't believe it.... It doesn't seem real.... I don't feel anything...."

Some people may interpret our shock as not caring. Others will compliment us on how well we are handling all of this. What these people don't realize is that we have yet to comprehend the immensity of our loss.

Even after the shock begins to wear off, there is a part of us that does not want to believe it is true. We may find ourselves talking to the person, and then remember that the person is no longer here. We may start to do something for the person that we had done every day, and then remember that the person no longer needs us to do that. We may find ourselves waiting for the person to call or come home at a specific time, and then remember that the person is not coming home.

Shock and disbelief are normal parts of the grieving process. It does not mean that we don't love the person. It does not mean that we don't care about the person.

This initial stage of grief does not usually last long. Eventually, we come to accept the reality that our loved one is gone and will not return. When that happens, we begin to feel the pain of separation. In the meantime, we can thank God for this strange frozen feeling that we are experiencing.

PRAYER: *Lord, I am feeling numb and disoriented. I can't believe that my loved one has died. It doesn't seem possible. I don't know what to do or where to turn, so I turn to you, Lord. Help me through this early stage of grief. Amen.*

✦✦✦✦✦

In The Year of Magical Thinking, *Joan Didion describes the numbing sensation that she felt immediately after the death of her husband: "I do not remember crying.... I had entered at the moment it happened[,] a kind of shock in which the only thought I allowed myself was that there must be certain things I needed to do."*

✦✦✦✦✦

3. Telling the Story

Give sorrow words; the grief that does not speak whispers
the o'er-fraught heart and bids it break.
— William Shakespeare

In the first days and weeks after the death of a loved one, we find ourselves telling the story of what happened over and over again. We talk about what happened, how it happened, why it happened, when it happened. We go over and over the details. Each time we tell the story, we bring ourselves another step closer to accepting the death.

We need to tell the story because there is still a part of us that does not want to believe that it happened. There is still a part of us that wants to believe it was all a bad dream.

Telling the story also helps the people we speak to. They undoubtedly heard about what happened, but they often don't know what to say to comfort us. Listening to the story of what happened is as much a relief for them as it is for us!

Problems arise a few weeks after the funeral, when the reality of the death hits us with full force. We still need to talk about it, but many of the people in our lives don't want to listen. They want us to go back to being the way we were before. They tell us that we have to move on with our lives. They already know the story, and they don't want to hear about our sorrow, our sadness, our pain, or our feelings of loss.

We know that we can turn to God in our sorrow. The psalmist assures us that "The LORD is close to the brokenhearted, / saves those whose spirit is crushed" (Ps 34:18). But when we are grieving, we are like the little child who told his mother, "I know God is with me at all times, but right now I need someone with skin!"

Talking to someone else about our grief is an important part of the grieving process. If we are having difficulty finding family members or friends who will listen, we may want to seek out the help of a bereavement support group or a bereavement counselor.

PRAYER: *Lord, I know that you are with me in my grief, but I need other people who will listen to my pain. Give me the courage to reach out and ask for the help I need. Allow me to see your face and hear your voice in the people who come to my aid. Amen.*

❧❧❧❧❧

"Real friends are those rare people who ask how you are and then wait to hear the answer." — Anonymous

"Comfort comes from knowing that people have made the same journey. And solace comes from understanding how others have learned to sing again." — Helen Steiner Rice

❧❧❧❧❧

4. Asking Why

There are occasions and causes,
why and wherefore, in all things.
— William Shakespeare

When a loved one dies, we often find ourselves plagued with questions: *Why did this person die? Why did it have to happen? Why now? Why did it happen in this way?*

We may get immediate answers to some of our questions if people who were present at the time of death can give us the details of what happened.

Other questions may not be answered for a while. We may have to wait for autopsy reports, medical records, or police reports.

Some of our "Why" questions may never be answered because the circumstances surrounding the death of our loved one remain a mystery.

Or we may find ourselves asking the question "Why?" but we really don't expect an answer. Our agonizing "Why ... Why ... Why ..." may be our protest over what has happened. Our tortured "Why" may be an expression of helplessness because we can't change what happened. Our heartbreaking "Why?" may be an articulation of our excruciating pain.

Asking "Why?" is an important part of the grieving process. It helps us to understand what happened. It helps us to accept the reality of what happened. It helps us to come to grips with what happened.

"Why" questions can also lead to something good. They can give us the impetus to right a wrong

14

or correct a harmful situation that could result in the death of someone else.

We may never get satisfying answers to our "Why" questions. We may always wonder — but over time, we can assure ourselves that the wondering will become less frustrating.

PRAYER: *Lord, I have so many questions. I want to give the questions to you. You already know the answers. Help me to accept that I may never receive answers to my questions. Help me to let go of this painful questioning. Amen.*

⥨⥨⥨⥨⥨

The Serenity Prayer, by Reinhold Niebuhr, can help us to put everything into perspective when we feel unsettled because of our "Why" questions:

> God grant me the serenity
> to accept the things I cannot change;
> courage to change the things I can;
> and wisdom to know the difference.

⥨⥨⥨⥨⥨

5. THE WAY WE GRIEVE

*My eyes are blind with anguish, /
and my whole frame is like a shadow.*
— JOB 17:7

HOW WE GRIEVE depends on a number of factors. When we suffer a major loss, our pattern of grieving may be similar to the way we grieved in the past, but with greater intensity. Our personalities, our relationship with the person who died, and our relationship with God all come into play.

We may grieve in the same way that we saw our parents grieve. Or we may find that our way of grieving is completely different.

Some of us deal with the grief by crying, while others of us find that we can't cry at all. Some of us will be private in our grief, while others will be more demonstrative. Some of us will turn to God for comfort, while others will find that prayer is difficult.

There is no right or wrong way to grieve. It is important for us to remember, however, that every loss — no matter how great or small — needs to be grieved.

It's easier to understand our grief if we imagine that when our loved one died, it was as if someone injected us with a massive amount of negative energy that entered into our bodies. The negative energy might feel like sadness, anger, loneliness, tension, or pain. Grieving is the process by which we find ways to get the negative energy out of our systems.

Getting the negative energy out doesn't mean that we stop loving the person. It doesn't mean that we stop missing the person.

The pain we feel today will gradually lose its intensity and release its grip on us. Our grieving will end eventually, and we will begin to see that it doesn't really matter how other people grieve. It doesn't matter how much anyone else is suffering. What matters is that we are experiencing the loss of an important person, and that we need this special time to heal in our own unique way.

PRAYER: *Lord, help me to grieve the loss of my loved one. Help me to understand that you never promised a life without pain or suffering, but you did promise that you would be with us always. Comfort me in my sadness; and when I feel as if I can't go on, carry me through the pain. Jesus, I trust in you. Amen.*

⇐⇐⇐⇐⇐

St. Thérèse of Lisieux describes her grief over the loss of her mother in these words:

> The moment Mummy died, my happy disposition changed completely. I had been lively and cheerful, but I became timid and quiet and a bundle of nerves. A glance was often enough to make me burst into tears. I was only happy if no one took notice of me, and I couldn't endure being with strangers.

⇐⇐⇐⇐⇐

6. Suppressing Grief

If you suppress grief too much, it can well redouble.
— Molière

THERE ARE MANY FACTORS involved in the suppression of grief. But no matter what the reason we have for denying, avoiding, ignoring, or postponing our grief, it is one of the biggest mistakes we can make.

We may do it in an attempt to avoid the pain or because we don't want to accept the reality of the death. We may try to postpone our grief because our lives are busy and we don't want to "waste" time dealing with it. We may feel pressured by others to get back to normal. We may get so caught up in helping family members or friends deal with their grief that we don't take time to work through our own sorrow.

The reality, however, is that grief does not go away on its own. It takes a tremendous amount of our energy to keep it locked away inside us. Eventually, whether we like it or not, the grief will resurface, and it is often more difficult to deal with delayed grief than it is to face it in the first place.

The word *bereavement* means "to be torn apart." When someone we love dies, it feels as if they have been torn out of our lives, and we are left with a gaping wound. Grieving is the process by which we allow that wound to heal.

Grieving is hard work. During our time of bereavement, we have to accept the reality of the loss, acknowledge the pain that is associated with our loss, adjust to life without our loved one, recreate that person in our memory, and begin to move into a new stage in our own lives.

We have to work through each one of these aspects of grief — and when we come out of our time of bereavement, thoughts of our loved one will no longer be as painful. We won't forget the person, and we will never stop loving or missing that person. We will be able to go on with our lives, carrying our loved one in a special place in our hearts, where no one can ever take them away from us again.

PRAYER: *Lord, I am afraid of the pain of grief. Be with me as I enter into this dark time in my life. Give me enough light so that I can always see the next step. Be my comfort. Be my guide. Be my strength. I cannot do this without you. Amen.*

❦❦❦❦❦

Warnings against suppressing grief have been passed down through the ages. The Roman poet Ovid (43 B.C.-A.D. 17) cautioned: "Suppressed grief suffocates, it rages within the breast, and is forced to multiply its strength."

An old Turkish proverb advises: "He who conceals his grief finds no remedy for it."

An Italian proverb predicts: "Grief pent up will burst the heart."

❦❦❦❦❦

7. Why Do I Feel Like This?

No one ever told me that grief feels so like fear....
The same fluttering in the stomach, the same restlessness,
the yawning. I keep swallowing. At times it feels like
being mildly drunk or concussed.
— C. S. Lewis

Grief is not an illness, but it can affect us physically. We may feel so fatigued that we border on the brink of exhaustion. We may complain about unusual aches in our muscles and joints. We may feel a tightness in our chests, a racing heart, or a lump in our throats. We may suffer from headaches and backaches. We may feel hot or cold.

Our breathing may change. Some of us will take shallow breaths. Some of us will unconsciously hold our breath. We may breathe too quickly, creating a feeling of faintness or dizziness. We may find that we are prone to deep sighs and yawning.

Because these physical symptoms of grief can weaken the immune system, we may be more prone to colds or infections. We may break out with a rash or realize that our hair is falling out.

Food can be a problem — we may eat too much or can't bear to eat at all. We may be bothered by noise, but silence may also seem unbearable. We may be plagued with feelings of anxiety. We may find that we wrinkle our brow or clench our teeth without even realizing what we are doing. We may find ourselves trembling.

As incredible as it may seem, all of these physical symptoms are normal for a grieving person. It is the body's physical response to the loss we have experienced. It is part of the pain we must experience as we adjust to life without our loved one.

The best advice is to be patient. Over time, the physical symptoms of grief should begin to diminish. If they persist at their original intensity, it is a good idea to see a doctor. In the meantime, turn to Jesus, who is the physician for our souls, and ask for his help and healing.

PRAYER: *Lord, have mercy on me. I am experiencing physical pain in response to the loss of my loved one. I believe that you have the power to comfort me, to console me, and to heal me. I beg you to touch my life with your healing love. Amen.*

One of the best ways to manage the physical symptoms of grief is to turn our breathing into a prayer. Start by taking slow, deep breaths and imagine that you are breathing in God's love. Then breathe out tension. Breathe in God's love, and breathe out pain. Breathe in God's love, and breathe out sadness. Breathe in God's love, and breathe out anything that is bothersome or troubling.

The beauty of the breathing prayer is that it can be done anytime, in any place, and no one even knows that we are praying. It calms and comforts.

8. TIME

Grief makes one hour ten....
— WILLIAM SHAKESPEARE

TIME PASSES SLOWLY when we're struggling with the pain of grief. We tell ourselves that we will be okay if we can just get through the next hour, the next half hour, the next fifteen minutes. There are moments, especially during the dark hours of the night, when time seems to stand still.

We may feel as if we have been locked in a prison of grief. We wonder how long it will last. We wonder if our life will ever go back to being normal again.

If we turn to Scripture, we recall Jesus announcing that he had come to "proclaim liberty to captives / and recovery of sight to the blind, / to let the oppressed go free, / and to proclaim a year acceptable to the Lord" (Lk 4:18-19).

What could those words possibly mean for us as we struggle through our grief? Can Jesus liberate us from the prison of grief that we find ourselves in? Can Jesus help us to see things differently? Can Jesus free us from the oppressive feelings of loss that we experience?

The answer is yes, but it won't happen instantaneously. Most bereavement experts agree it takes a full year to work through the pain of losing a loved one. Throughout the year, the raw feelings of grief eventually give way to a more aching kind of grief. The whole purpose of grieving is to move us to a place where memories are no longer painful and we can continue with our lives.

Do we have enough faith to believe that Jesus can help us through this painful process? Can we believe that throughout our time of bereavement we will begin to see things in a new way? Can we trust that the Lord will give us the strength we need?

Maybe we need to look at our time of grieving as "a year acceptable to the Lord."

PRAYER: *Lord, strengthen my faith as I move through this time of grief. Help me to see that feelings of grief will rise and fall at different levels of intensity for months. Allow me to rely on you for the comfort and courage I need to move through the prison of grief. Amen.*

It wasn't until years after the death of her mother that St. Thérèse of Lisieux described in her spiritual autobiography, The Story of a Soul, how the Lord consoled her in her grief:

> *God's little flower would never have survived if He had not poured his warmth and light on her. She was still too frail to stand up to rain and storm. She needed warmth, the gently dropping dew and the soft airs of spring. She was never without them, for Jesus gave them to her, even amidst the bleak winter of her suffering.*

9. THE GIFT OF TEARS

Jesus wept.
— JOHN 11:35

THE PROBLEM WITH TEARS is that we never know when something will trigger an emotional response in us. It might be a song on the radio, or an image that pops into our heads, or something that someone says.

There are times when tears simply start to flow, and we don't even know why. Our eyes fill up, and we feel self-conscious, especially if we are around people who are not comfortable with tears. We may try to stop ourselves from crying, or we may rush off to a private place where we can break down. We may think of tears as our enemy, as something bad, something that embarrasses us, something that requires an apology.

When we look at the Scriptures, however, we discover that Jesus wept openly when his friend Lazarus died (Jn 11:35). Jesus did not try to hide his sadness. He was not embarrassed by his emotions. He did not apologize or run off. Jesus simply wept, and in doing so, he gave us permission to weep over the loss of someone we love.

Tears are an important part of the grieving process. A study by Dr. William H. Frey II, a biochemist at the St. Paul-Ramsey Medical Centre in Minnesota, found that the tears of a grieving person have a chemical makeup that is different from the tears of someone who is slicing onions. Tears are God's way of allowing us to release the toxins that build up in our bodies during times of grief. Tears of grief are actually good for us.

After a good cry, we feel calmness in the depths of our being. It's almost as if the built-up emotions have suddenly flushed out in our flood of tears. Our hearts feel less heavy. The grief we have been carrying is a little lighter.

Many of the greatest saints refer to tears as a gift. Tears cleanse our emotions the same way the waters of baptism cleanse our souls. Our tears are holy. Our tears have meaning and purpose. Our tears are a gift from a gracious and loving God who knows the depths of our pain.

So the next time our eyes flood with tears, we can simply say to those around us, "I need to cry for a moment because tears help to restore my strength and my spirit." We don't have to apologize. We don't have to feel embarrassed. Going off to a private place is okay. But we may discover that, like Jesus, our ability to weep openly gives others permission to cry. And we may find that the people who share our grief will begin to recognize that their tears are a gift too.

PRAYER: *Lord, help me to appreciate the gift of tears. Give me the courage to accept my tears. Allow my tears to release some of the sadness that I feel. Allow my tears to wash away some of the pain. And after my tears have ended, Lord, give me blessed calm. Amen.*

❤❤❤❤❤

"There is a sacredness in tears. They are not the mark of weakness, but of power. They speak more eloquently than ten thousand tongues. They are messengers of overwhelming grief, of deep contrition, and of unspeakable love." — *Washington Irving*

❤❤❤❤❤

10. The Problem of Sleep

Where you used to be, there is a hole in the world,
which I find myself constantly walking around in the
daytime, and falling into at night.
— Edna St. Vincent Millay

Sleep is one of our greatest challenges when we are
grieving. During the daytime, when we are supposed
to be active and alert, we often feel as if we are forcing ourselves to keep going when all we really want
is to escape into a deep sleep. At night, we often
lie awake, plagued by thoughts or memories. We are
like the psalmist who wrote:

> You have kept me from closing my eyes in sleep;
>   I am troubled and cannot speak.
> I consider the days of old;
>   the years long past I remember. (Ps 77:5-6)

We know that we need to sleep. We know that
sleep will restore us. But we toss and turn in a useless
attempt to drift off. Or we may fall asleep, only to
awaken from a vivid dream about our loved one, and
we find it impossible to get back to sleep again. We
are left with feelings of complete exhaustion.

It's important to remember that the Lord urges
us, "Come to me, all you who labor and are bur-
dened, and I will give you rest" (Mt 11:28).

When we're having difficulty falling asleep, it
helps if we can use our imagination to place ourselves in the arms of the Lord. We can imagine that
the Lord is comforting us in our grief. We can close

our eyes and repeat to ourselves, "I am resting with the Lord.... I am resting with the Lord...."

In this way, we can turn our difficulties with sleep into a special kind of prayer.

PRAYER: *Lord, I need you to be with me through the darkness of the night. Allow me to rest in you. I am weary, and I need your comfort and your strength. Jesus, I trust in you. Amen.*

❧❧❧❧❧

Bereavement experts offer the following advice for people who are having trouble with sleep:

- ❧ *Get up at the same time every morning, even if you haven't slept.*
- ❧ *Exercise during the day so that you will be tired by bedtime.*
- ❧ *Cut down on your caffeine intake.*
- ❧ *Don't use alcohol as a sleep aid. It is a depressant, but the effects wear off after a few hours and leave you restless in the middle of the night.*
- ❧ *Relax before bedtime with music, quiet prayer, a bath, or spiritual reading.*
- ❧ *If you can't fall asleep after twenty minutes of trying, get up and do something until you feel tired. Then try again.*

❧❧❧❧❧

11. FEELING CRUSHED

The LORD is close to the brokenhearted, / saves those whose spirit is crushed.
— PSALM 34:19

GRIEF CAN FEEL LIKE a great weight that bears down on us. We may feel trapped or unable to move — almost as if a paralyzing force has taken hold of us.

Grief is crushing our spirits. We are like grapes that have been plucked from the vine and thrown into a large vat, where we are smashed and left to ferment.

Grief is changing us. We don't like feeling this way. We know that we will never be the same as we were before. But in this process of being crushed and fermented, we have a choice. We can come out of our grief as wine or we can come out of our grief as vinegar.

If we choose to become wine, we will come out of our grief with grace, with beauty, and with a mellowness that comes from suffering through a devastating loss and surviving. We will once again be able to appreciate life, and others will appreciate what we have become. Our lives will have new meaning and purpose.

If we choose to become vinegar, we will come out of our grief embittered, resentful, angry, and close to despair. We will find that our appreciation for life has soured, and others will find it unpleasant to be around us. Our lives will have a new meaning, but it will be harsh and biting.

We did not choose for our loved one to die. We did not choose for our spirits to be crushed. But we do have choices as to the outcome. Will we invite God into our grief? Will we ask him to make us wine? Or will we choose to become vinegar?

PRAYER: *Lord, grieving is so painful. My heart is broken. My spirit is crushed. Help me through this process so that I can find new meaning and purpose in my life. I don't want to come out of this embittered. I believe that you can save me with your healing love. Amen.*

"God of our life, there are days when the burdens we carry chafe our shoulders and weigh us down; when the road seems dreary and endless, the skies grey and threatening; when our lives have no music in them, and our hearts are lonely, and our souls have lost their courage. Flood the path with light, run our eyes to where the skies are full of promise; tune our hearts to brave music; give us the sense of comradeship with heroes and saints of every age; and so quicken our spirits that we may be able to encourage the souls of all who journey with us on the road of life, to your honor and glory." — St. Augustine

12. Feeling Crazy

Grief teaches the steadiest minds to waver.
— Sophocles

WHEN WE GRIEVE the loss of a loved one we sometimes feel as if we are going crazy. Everything seems unsettled. We have trouble concentrating. We are forgetful. We feel confused. Nothing seems to make sense in the way it did before.

We may find ourselves talking to our loved one. We may think we hear our loved one's voice. We may cling to objects or articles of clothing that belonged to our loved one. We may feel the presence of our loved one, and then realize that no one is there.

There are times when we fall back into old habits, like setting a place for the person at the table, or buying something that we know our loved one would appreciate. We may feel the need to leave a light on at night. We may think we see our loved one but then realize that we were mistaken. We may dream about our loved one, and believe with all our heart that our dream was real.

We have to assure ourselves that these kinds of behaviors, which may seem abnormal, are actually an important part of the grieving process. These things happen because our minds are still trying to comprehend that our loved one is not coming back. We are not crazy. We are grieving, and it's okay.

We can cope with the craziness by concentrating on doing little things that feel normal — cleaning out a drawer, fixing something that is broken, taking a walk, praying a decade of the Rosary, or doing something nice for someone else.

The crazy stage will eventually end, and we will move into another phase of the grieving process. In the meantime, we can assure ourselves that we are not losing our minds.

PRAYER: *Lord, sometimes I feel as if I am losing my mind. Nothing is the way it used to be. I don't know what to say or do. Be my anchor in this time of turmoil. Allow me to cling to you for support and for safety. I can't go through this on my own. Amen.*

❦❦❦❦❦

After the death of her daughter, St. Elizabeth Anne Seton admitted that for six months she felt as if she was losing her mind: "After Nina was taken I was so often expecting to lose my senses, and my head was so disordered that unless for the daily duties always before me, I did not know much of what I did or what I had left undone."

❦❦❦❦❦

13. Making Decisions

*There is an appointed time for everything, / and a time
for every affair under the heavens.*
— Ecclesiastes 3:1

One of the problems we face in our time of bereavement is that we are thrust into a position of having to make decisions at a time when we are the least capable of making them. We have to make decisions about the wake, the funeral, the cemetery or mausoleum, a gravestone, or some other kind of memorial.

The decisions that come after the funeral, however, are often the most difficult and potentially harmful. These are the decisions that will impact our future.

When we are confronted with these major decisions, we need to take our time. We should not allow anyone to pressure us or rush us into doing something that we may end up regretting. Most experts agree that we need to wait at least a year before making any permanent change in our lives.

We need this time to adjust to life without our loved one. We need this time to examine all the pros and cons of a major decision. We need this time to consult with experts who can help us to make informed decisions. We need this time to heal.

It's a good idea, for instance, to visit family members off and on for a full year before making the permanent decision to sell our home and move in with them. We should ask our employers for a leave of absence, rather than abruptly quitting our jobs. We should experience life without our loved one for a while before we decide to have another child or marry another person. We should find out how much it actually costs us to live before we begin selling stocks and liquidating assets.

All of these matters have a tremendous impact on our future. Nothing is so urgent that it can't wait for a while. There's an old saying, "No winter lasts forever; no spring skips its turn."

Perhaps the best advice comes from St. Francis de Sales, who says: "The slow cure is always the surest.... So we must be brave and patient."

PRAYER: *Lord, be with me through the turmoil of decision-making in the aftermath of the death of my loved one. You know how difficult life is for me right now. Help me to be brave and patient. And when the time comes for me to make decisions, guide me so that I will choose what is right and what is good. Amen.*

Lynn Caine, author of Widow, *offers the following advice for grieving people who are faced with major decisions:*

> *During my crazy periods, I made terrible financial mistakes. That's why I keep repeating my advice to widows. Sit down. Be quiet. Don't move. You have to understand that your mind is not working properly, even though you think it is. Protect yourself from yourself.*

14. Helping Ourselves

Heaven ne'er helps the men who will not act.
— Sophocles

THE PAIN OF GRIEF can be so overwhelming at times that we sometimes wonder if we will ever be able to get through this. The answer is yes, but we can't just sit and wait for our grief to end. Grief is a natural process, but it is our responsibility to do whatever we can to make the grieving process easier.

We can start by taking good care of ourselves. The stress we experience as part of the grieving process takes a tremendous physical toll on our bodies. It's a good idea to drink a lot of water and take a multivitamin daily.

We also have to watch what we eat. Eating a lot of junk food may seem like a comfort when we're doing it, but it provides little nutritional value and can actually decrease our energy. Too much caffeine can keep us awake at night. Alcohol is a depressant that may make us feel tired, but it will not help us to get a good night's sleep — and it usually makes us feel worse in the morning. There's an old Chinese proverb that warns, "Just as a medicine may not cure a serious illness, wine will certainly not dispel your grief."

Exercise is more important than many of us realize. It makes us feel stronger. It relieves anxiety and stress. It tires us out so that we can sleep better at night. Exercise can be something as simple as walking or as structured as joining a gym or exercise class. (Please check with your health-care provider before starting a new dietary or exercise program.) After the death of his wife, C. S. Lewis admitted, "I do all the walking I can, for I'd be a fool to go to bed not tired."

We also have to set limits on what we do. This is not the time to take on extra responsibilities. We are shouldering a heavy burden of grief, so we may need to lighten our daily schedule. In the olden days, society recognized the need to grieve. People wore outward symbols of mourning. Women dressed in black. Men wore black armbands. Expectations for a grieving person were lowered.

Today, we don't have that advantage. We have to take care of ourselves as we move through the grieving process. We have to let people know that we are going through a difficult time. We have to ask God to help us, but we also have to put some effort into it. As the old adage says, "God helps those who help themselves."

PRAYER: *Lord, I didn't realize that grief would be so difficult. I know that you will help me if I do what is necessary to help myself. Give me the courage to express my needs to others. Help me to say no when things are overwhelming. Fill me with hope that better days lie ahead. Amen.*

❅❅❅❅❅

One of the earliest sources of the saying "God helps those who help themselves" comes from Aesop's Fables. As the story goes, a man with a wagon was driving on a muddy road. When the wagon wheels began to sink, he jumped down from the wagon, prayed for help, and heard a voice from the sky saying, "Don't just kneel there. Get up and push the wheel!"

❅❅❅❅❅

15. THE MYSTERY OF DEATH

What is death? I do not know, and you do not know.
— HENRI NOUWEN

WHETHER OR NOT we were with our loved one at the moment of death, we often wonder what happens when someone passes from this life to the next. We know that at the moment of death, our souls separate from our bodies, but we don't know how this happens. Just before Jesus died, he said: "Father, into your hands I commend my spirit" (Lk 23:46). We know that in Scripture the same word that is used for soul, or spirit, is also used for breath. Did our loved ones breathe out their soul with their last breath?

We wonder if accounts of near-death experiences — with tunnels, lights, and feelings of overwhelming peace — are true. We wonder if deceased family members or friends were waiting for our loved one.

We know from Scripture that Jesus promised to be present at the moment of our death: "I will come back again and take you to myself, so that where I am you also may be" (Jn 14:3). We wonder if Jesus was waiting for our loved one.

There is no way we will know for certain what happens until we pass from this life to the next at the moment of our own death. We do know that when we were born, we came out of the safety of our mother's womb into a world where people were waiting for us. Do we have enough faith to believe that the same thing happens at the moment of death?

Perhaps the words of St. Bernard of Clairvaux will help: "I believe though I do not comprehend, and I hold by faith what I cannot grasp with the mind."

Death is a mystery, and it is only through faith that we can be comforted and assured.

PRAYER: *Lord, I can't help but wonder what happened to my loved one at the moment of death. I am afraid of what will happen when I die. Strengthen my faith. Help me to believe that you have prepared a place for us, and that I will be with my deceased loved ones for all eternity. Amen.*

❧❧❧❧❧

"If it was properly explained that death was nothing but going home to God, then there would be no fear of death."
— *Blessed Mother Teresa of Calcutta*

❧❧❧❧❧

16. Where Is God?

God is nearer to us than we think.
— Brother Lawrence

AFTER THE DEATH of a loved one, some of us gain comfort and strength from our faith in God. But for others of us, it feels as if God has become more distant. We want God to comfort us. We want God to calm our fears, to answer our questions, and to take away our pain. But we don't feel God's presence. So we begin to ask ourselves, "Where is God?"

Jesus asked the same question when he hung on the cross. He felt as if God had abandoned him. His agonizing plea was actually the opening lines of Psalm 22:

> My God, my God, why have you abandoned me?
>> Why so far from my call for help,
>> from my cries of anguish?
> My God, I call by day, but you do not answer;
>> by night, but I have no relief. (vv. 2-3)

If we read a little further in the psalm, we find that the words quickly change from a desperate question to a plea for God's assistance: "Do not stay far from me, / for trouble is near, / and there is no one to help" (v. 12).

Toward the end, the psalmist promises to praise God forever: "For he has not spurned or disdained the misery of this poor wretch, / Did not turn away from me, but heard me when I cried out" (v. 25).

When we begin to question the presence of God in the midst of our own grief, we need to follow the example of Jesus and the psalmist by begging God to help us. We need to remind ourselves that God is always with us — even if we can't feel his presence.

The time will come when we will feel God's presence again. In the meantime, we have to keep calling out to him. We have to ask him to help us through this difficult time. We must believe that we are not alone.

PRAYER: *Lord, I don't feel your presence. I feel so alone, so lost, so sad. Even though I don't feel you with me, I believe that you are here. Help me through this dark time in my life. I cannot do this on my own. Amen.*

❮❮❮❮❮

There's an ancient Indian story about a father, who took his son into the forest for a rite of passage that would transform the boy into a man. He asked his son to sit on a rock. Then he blindfolded the boy and told him that he had to sit there alone and in silence throughout the night. The boy was told not remove the blindfold until dawn. If the boy survived, it would be proof that he was now a man.

The boy spent the night in terror. He could hear the sounds of animals around him, but he sat there as his father had instructed. In the morning, he removed the blindfold and saw his father sitting on a nearby stone. The father had been there throughout the night, protecting his son from harm, even though the boy did not realize that he was there.

❮❮❮❮❮

17. Who Am I?

I have trouble thinking of myself as a widow.
— Joan Didion

When someone who was an important part of our lives is no longer with us, we lose a part of our identity. So much of who we are was interwoven with that person in a bond of love. Suddenly, we are no longer that person's spouse ... or mother ... child ... sibling ... friend ... caretaker.

The things we used to do for or with that person can no longer be done. The hopes and dreams we shared are ended. We feel lost. We have no sense of purpose or direction. There is a large void in our lives, and we don't know how we can live with this emptiness.

Our normal routines no longer make sense. We don't know what to do because that important person in our lives is no longer with us. Everything that happens reminds us of our loss. We find it hard to comprehend how the rest of the world can go on as if nothing happened when it feels like our world is falling apart.

When we struggle with the question of who we are now that our loved one is gone, we plunge ourselves into two of the most difficult parts of the grieving process: we suffer the pain of our loss, and at the same time, we begin to adjust to life without the presence of the person we love. Our pain is great because our love was so profound.

We have to remind ourselves that struggling with our identity is part of the grieving process. It helps if we can recognize that we are grief-stricken people who are trying to come to grips with a difficult loss.

Our new identity will evolve, and we will find new meaning in our lives. But we have to give ourselves time to heal. As part of the healing process, we will begin to experience new things. New people will enter our lives. We will be the same person that we always were, but we will grow into a different understanding of our meaning and purpose in life. It just takes time. So the best thing we can do is to be patient with ourselves.

PRAYER: *Lord, I feel so lost. I don't know who I am or what I should be doing from one minute to the next. Be with me, Lord. Take my hand and guide me through this difficult time. I need your help. I cannot do this without you. Amen.*

"When we mourn, we die to something that gives us a sense of who we are. In this sense suffering always has much to do with the spiritual life. We surrender our striving denial of our limitations. We release our hold on a piece of our identity as a spouse, a parent, as a member of a church, as a resident of a community or nation." — Henri Nouwen

18. Memories

Joy and grief are in conflict in my heart.
It is a delight to recall such a man;
to be deprived of his presence is a deep sorrow.
— St. Hilary of Arles

WE CLING TO MEMORIES of our loved ones after they die. There's an old saying that God allows us to remember so that we can have roses in December. God also allows us to remember our loved ones so that we can carry them with us in our hearts.

We remember the things they said and did. We remember their laughter, the twinkle in their eyes, their advice, their warnings, their questions, their stories, and their concerns.

The problem with memories is that after a while the sharpness of our memories starts to fade.

C. S. Lewis described his own angst as memories of his wife became less focused: "We have seen the faces of those we know best so variously, from so many angles, in so many lights, with so many expressions — waking, sleeping, laughing, crying, eating, talking, thinking — that all the impressions crowd into our memory together and cancel into a mere blur."

Some of us try to preserve the memories of our loved ones by creating a memory book with things that our loved ones said or did. Some of us put together photo albums. Some of us keep a treasure box with some of our loved ones' possessions. These kinds of things are all helpful. It helps us adjust to the reality that our loved ones are no longer physically present to us.

As living memories begin to fade, we find ourselves planting deep within our hearts loving memories that no one can ever take away. These memories will surface from time to time. We will recall not only the things our loved ones said or did, but we will also feel their presence deep inside us — and even if it brings tears, it will also bring comfort and consolation.

PRAYER: *Lord, give me the courage to accept that the living memories of my loved ones will begin to fade with time. Help me to move the memories of my loved ones from my head into my heart, where I can carry them with me forever. Amen.*

❅❅❅❅❅

"I know for certain that we never lose the people we love, even to death. They continue to participate in every act, thought and decision we make. Their love leaves an indelible imprint in our memories. We find comfort in knowing that our lives have been enriched by having shared their love."
— *Leo Buscaglia*

❅❅❅❅❅

19. SADNESS

In this sad world of ours, sorrow comes to all, and it
often comes with bitter agony. Perfect relief is not
possible, except with time. You cannot now believe that
you will ever feel better. But this is not true. You are sure
to be happy again. Knowing this, truly believing it,
will make you less miserable now. I have
had enough experience to make this statement.
— ABRAHAM LINCOLN

IT IS OFTEN DIFFICULT for us to describe the sadness
that we feel after the death of a loved one. At times
it feels like an ache. Other times it feels like longing.
We may feel like a heavy weight is pressing on our
hearts. It may feel like a stabbing pain. Sometimes
we feel as if we are trapped in a cloud of gloom.

We hear people refer to the sadness of grief as
"depression." While we may experience some of the
same symptoms as someone who is depressed, the
sadness of grief and clinical depression are, techni-
cally, not the same.

When we are grieving, we are sad — but we are
not sad all of the time. The sadness of grief still allows us to experience moments of pleasure. We can
still appreciate the beauty of nature, the love of a
child, and the comfort of a pet. We can feel empathy
for other people. We can smile and laugh when we
think back on things our loved one said or did —
even if our laughter is mixed with tears.

We can still function in the sadness of our
grief. Many of us still go to work and take care of
our homes and families — even though some days
are more difficult than others. Sadness is a normal

part of the grieving process. It's okay to express our sadness to other people. It's okay to say, "Today is a sad day for me."

Some experts suggest that we set aside a certain time every day to allow ourselves to feel sad. Whether our sad time is in the morning or later in the day, we know that we can get through the rest of the day because we have set aside time to grieve. In time, our sadness will begin to lessen. It won't mean that we no longer care about what happened to our loved one. It means that the raw emotions associated with our grief are starting to heal.

PRAYER: *Lord, today is a sad day for me. I feel the weight of sadness in every part of my being. I need your help. Comfort me in my sadness. Bring me a sense of calming peace. Amen.*

❧❧❧❧❧

Some comforting words for sad days come from Blessed John XXIII:

> *Every day I need you, Lord, but this day especially I need some extra strength to face whatever is to be.... This day more than any other day I need to feel you near, to fortify my courage and to overcome my fear. By myself, I cannot meet the challenge of the hour. There are times when human creatures need a higher Power to help them bear what must be borne. And so, dear Lord, I pray that you will hold on to my trembling hand and be with me today.*

❧❧❧❧❧

20. ANGER

My tongue will tell the anger of my heart, or else my heart concealing it will break.
— WILLIAM SHAKESPEARE

WE KNOW THAT one of the normal stages of grief is anger, but we don't always know how to deal with our anger or how to express it. It helps if we recognize anger as an emotional response to something we perceive as unfair or unjust.

We may feel angry because our loved one died. Or anger may well up in us because this death seems unfair. Maybe the death was unexpected. Maybe the death happened at the worst possible time or in the worst possible way. It doesn't matter why we feel the death was unjust; the result is that we feel angry.

Sometimes, we feel angry with our loved one. We may know that our feelings are irrational, but we feel angry because it feels as if our loved one has abandoned us. We feel angry because we don't know what to do. We feel angry because we can't discuss this with our loved one. We feel angry because we have to go through all of this alone.

We may feel angry with God because he allowed our loved one to die. We may have been praying for a miracle that did not happen. We may feel that God should have protected our loved one. We may feel that God could have done something to prevent this. It seems wrong. We did not deserve this.

Experts agree that the best thing we can do with our anger is to express it. Keeping anger bottled up inside us only leads to resentment. We have to get the anger out. We can do that by talking about it or crying about it. Some people find that physical activity is a good outlet for anger. Writing about anger in a journal is another good way to release anger.

Prayer can be a real help when we pour out our feelings to God. God knows we are angry, so a prayer that comes from the depths of our hearts is one of the most profound prayers that we can experience.

PRAYER: *Lord, you know how angry I am because of the death of my loved one. Help me to work through this anger. Allow me to find an outlet for my anger so that my anger does not turn into bitterness and resentment. I believe that you are with me. I believe that you will help me in my grief. Amen.*

❧❧❧❧❧

Psychologists James D. Whitehead and Evelyn Eaton Whitehead suggest that sometimes our anger is trying to tell us something, and that it helps if we can discover the message in our anger:

> *Discerning this message requires effort. We stop to reflect on what triggers our angry feelings; we interrupt a customary pattern of response to ask what needs to be questioned or challenged or set aside. Evaluating our anger inserts a pause in our arousal, leaving space for anger's wisdom to emerge.*

❧❧❧❧❧

21. BLAME

Great tranquility of heart is his who cares
for neither praise nor blame.
— THOMAS À KEMPIS

WHEN BAD THINGS HAPPEN, we often look for someone to blame. We may blame our loved one for behaviors that ultimately resulted in death. We look at a history of smoking, drinking, drugs, lack of exercise, weight gain or loss, depression, not seeing a doctor, ignoring symptoms, and seemingly not caring about health or life.

We may have good reason to place blame on someone or something else. Tragic deaths that occur because of violence, drunkenness, negligence, or neglect are certainly deserving of our blame. Deaths caused by greed, pollution, and unethical business practices also deserve blame.

But sometimes we don't have anyone to blame for what happened to our loved one. Death came because of an accident, an act of nature, or a malfunctioning of the person's own body. When this happens, it's really no one's fault, but we may still want to find someone that we can point a finger at and say, "You caused this to happen!" We may be tempted to blame the rescue workers, the paramedics, the doctors, the nurses, or other people who were trying to help but could not save our loved one's life.

The irony is that whether the blame is justified or not, blame does not bring back our loved one. We don't feel a sense of relief because we can say, "You did this! You are responsible." If we allow our feelings of blame to fester inside us, we can become bitter and resentful.

The only way something good can come from blame is when we channel our blame into action so that the same thing does not happen to someone else. When we do this, we transform our blame into something positive and worthwhile.

We can also ask God to help us let go of our desire to blame. Richard Rohr, O.F.M., suggests that we ask God to help us transform our blame so that we can one day say, "I should be blaming or bitter, but because of God and grace, I am not."

PRAYER: *Lord, I want to blame someone or something for the death of my loved one, but I know that blame will only make me bitter and resentful. Give me the courage to turn my feelings of blame over to you. I believe that you can transform my desire to blame into something good and holy. Amen.*

❅❅❅❅❅

There are thousands of examples of how people have transformed feelings of blame into positive actions that worked toward correcting an injustice or preventing the deaths of others. One of the most famous was the work of Candy Lightner, who founded Mothers Against Drunk Driving in 1980, after her daughter was killed by a repeat drunk-driving offender. You may want to think how you can focus your indignation over the death of your loved into something positive.

❅❅❅❅❅

22. Regrets

Regret is an appalling waste of energy;
you can't build on it; it's only for wallowing in.
— KATHERINE MANSFIELD

ONE OF THE MOST PAINFUL aspects of grief is that we don't have the opportunity to talk with our loved one again. We may anguish over angry words that were spoken before our loved one died. We may struggle with promises that were not kept. We may be sorry for things that we did. We may chastise ourselves for not having done more.

We may feel terrible because we did not recognize signs that the person was dying. We may wish we had insisted that our loved one go to the doctor. We may be sorry that we did not prepare healthier foods or encourage healthier habits. We may wish that we could move back in time and do things differently. We may feel as if we are filled with regret, and our regret intensifies the pain of our grief.

The worst thing we can do is to allow those feelings of regret to fester inside us. We need to talk about our feelings of guilt with a friend, with a spiritual adviser, or with a priest. We may come to the realization that what we did or did not do made no difference in what happened. We may come to see that we did what we thought was right at the time. Or we may admit to ourselves that we may not have taken the best course of action but recognize that there was no malice in our actions. Then we have to let it go.

St. Augustine tells us, "Entrust the past to God's mercy, the present to his love, the future to his providence."

We can do that by turning to God to express our regrets, admit to God that we are sorry for what happened, and then believe with all of our heart that we have been forgiven.

PRAYER: *Lord, you know that I carry so many regrets in my heart. I am deeply sorry for the things I may have said or done to hurt my loved one. Free me from my guilt. Help me to believe that I have been forgiven by you and by my loved one. Amen.*

The Sacrament of Reconciliation is another avenue for helping us to wash away any guilt, regret, remorse, or shame that we may feel because of something that happened in the past. You can go into a confessional or make a private appointment with a priest to discuss the matter.

In the sacrament, you will not only hear the comforting words of absolution, but you will also receive the grace you need to help you put an end to your torment. There is an old saying that God can only mend a broken heart when he is given all the pieces.

23. Forgiveness

He who knows how to forgive prepares for himself
many graces from God.
— St. Faustina Kowalska

Sometimes, the relationships with our loved ones were complicated. A loved one may have said or done things that hurt us, and we never reconciled during the person's life. Maybe that person asked for our forgiveness and we refused. Maybe that person never realized how hurt we were.

Maybe we didn't discover something about our loved one until after he or she died, and the secret devastated us.

We may feel hurt, angry, or betrayed, but we no longer have the opportunity to deal with the person and whatever happened. These kinds of conflicts intensify our grief. We are left with a choice: we can hold on to our feelings of anger and resentment, or we can choose to forgive the person for what happened.

Forgiveness after death is possible. But first, we have to understand the nature of forgiveness. Our ability to forgive does not depend on how we feel about the person or what the person did. Forgiveness is part of our free will. Forgiveness is a choice.

When we forgive, we make a clear, free choice to let go of anger, resentment, and feelings of betrayal. The person may not deserve our forgiveness, but we choose to forgive anyway because forgiveness frees us from pain and bitterness.

When the person we want to forgive has died, we have to tell God that we want to forgive, and then leave the matter in the Lord's hands.

We can ease the process of forgiveness by talking with a priest or counselor. We can write a letter to the person we are forgiving, and then burn it or bury it at the cemetery. We can also show that our intentions to forgive are serious by praying for the person who has died. It will be a sign to God that we truly want to forgive, and we will find peace in knowing that God will help us to let go of the pain.

PRAYER: *Lord, you know the complexities of my relationship with my loved one. Give me the courage to forgive and to seek forgiveness even though I can no longer speak directly with this person. You know the workings of my heart and soul. Help me to let go of any negative feelings. Give me the graces I need to move beyond this dreadful hurt. Amen.*

⇐⇐⇐⇐⇐

"When I talk of forgiveness I mean the belief that you can come out the other side a better person. A better person than the one being consumed by anger and hatred. Remaining in that state locks you in a state of victimhood, making you almost dependent on the perpetrator. If you can find it in yourself to forgive, then you are no longer chained to the perpetrator. You can move on...." — *Desmond Tutu*

⇐⇐⇐⇐⇐

24. Fear

You gain strength, courage, and confidence by
every experience in which you really stop
to look fear in the face.
— Eleanor Roosevelt

When we're grieving, feelings of fear often take us by surprise. We expect feelings of sadness. We don't expect fear, and yet we often find ourselves feeling afraid. We may have specific fears about finances or how we will go on with our lives. We may fear that we will not be able to do everything that needs to be done. We feel uncertain of what the future will bring. We may be afraid that someone else will die. We may fear our own death.

Fear drains our energy and distorts our perception of reality. Our fear of what might happen is almost always worse than what actually unfolds. The best thing we can do is talk about our fears. When we verbalize our fears, they begin to lose their power over us, and we discover that other people can help us move through the difficulties we face.

Our goal should be to stay in the present moment. God gives us the strength to get through what is happening now. When we worry about the future, we miss the grace of the present. We need to say to ourselves, "I can't worry about tomorrow. With God's help I can get through today!"

One problem we may encounter is that fear sometimes comes back disguised as doubt. We may hear a little voice inside us saying, "You're not going to be able to get through this." When this happens, we have to stand firm. We will be able to get through this, and there are people in our lives who can help us! We are not alone!

We can also trust that God will be with us every step of the way. We have to listen to the voice of God in Scripture: "Do not fear: I am with you; / do not be anxious: I am your God. / I will strengthen you, I will help you, / I will uphold you with my victorious right hand" (Is 41:10).

PRAYER: *Lord, you know that I struggle with many fears. I know that these fears are only making things worse. Help me to believe that you are with me. Take my hand and walk with me as I face my fears. Give me the strength and the courage to go on. Amen.*

❦❦❦❦

St. Francis de Sales offers the following advice to people who are afraid:

> *Do not look forward in fear to the changes of life;*
> *Rather look to them with full hope that as they arise,*
> *God, whose very own you are,*
> *will lead you safely through all things;*
> *And when you cannot stand it,*
> *God will carry you in His arms.*
> *Do not fear what may happen tomorrow;*
> *The same everlasting Father who cares for you today*
> *will take care of you today and every day.*
> *He will either shield you from suffering*
> *or will give you unfailing strength to bear it.*
> *Be at peace and put aside all anxious thoughts and*
>   *imaginations.*

❦❦❦❦❦

25. Loneliness

Pray that your loneliness may spur you into finding something to live for.
— DAG HAMMARSKJÖLD

WE EXPERIENCE TWO KINDS of loneliness in our grief. The first is the ache we feel when we miss the person we love. It is the pain of eating alone. It is tension we feel when we have to make decisions by ourselves. It is the emptiness we feel when we reach a birthday, an anniversary, or a special holiday, and our loved one is not there to share it. It is the aloneness we feel in the midst of a crowd. It is the longing that we experience in the middle of the night.

This kind of loneliness is part of the grieving process. It is through these feelings of separation and loneliness that we begin to adjust to the reality that our loved one is no longer physically present to us. It is a difficult process in which we learn to be alone.

The second kind of loneliness comes when we isolate ourselves from other people. We feel so sad that we sometimes build walls that keep other people from entering into our grief. We don't want to go out. We don't want to interact with anyone. C. S. Lewis described this kind of loneliness as: "A sort of invisible blanket between the world and me. I find it hard to take in what anyone says. Or perhaps, hard to want to take it in."

We can't deny loneliness. We have to feel the pain of loneliness before we can move on with our lives. But there are several things that we can do that can make the process a little easier.

We can unite our loneliness with the loneliness of Christ. We can use our imagination to join him in the Garden of Gethsemane. We can weep with him and admit that we are experiencing a kind of agony. Or we can go to a Eucharistic Adoration chapel to simply sit in the presence of the Lord. Many parishes now have twenty-four-hour adoration, so we can go at any time of the day or night.

Last, but not least, we can move outside of our loneliness by seeking out other people who are lonely. We can invite someone to share a meal. We can volunteer to help others. We can sign up for a class or join an exercise group. We can offer to bring someone to church. Reaching out to God and to other people is often what we need in order to break through the loneliness of grief.

PRAYER: *Lord, I feel so alone. Help me to ease the pain of loneliness. Give me the courage to reach outside of myself. Give me the strength to move beyond loneliness and find new meaning and purpose in my life. Amen.*

❖❖❖❖❖

Servant of God Catherine de Hueck Doherty, the founder of Madonna House, offered the following cure for loneliness:

> *There are moments in the depths of the night when we see, for a second, the sun shining brightly on everything, and beckoning us to become human. Cease to be alone. Begin to love. Begin to get involved with others. Begin to love your neighbor. Suddenly you understand that it is the Son who is talking to you; it is God who is calling you to get out of the morass of your loneliness.... Touch someone with the speech of your lips. Break the loneliness of others, and you will never be lonely again. Did you ever go into the nursing homes for senior citizens? There are whole floors of lonely people. Do something about it. Do something for others.*

❖❖❖❖❖

26. Secondary Losses

*To have courage for whatever comes
in life — everything lies in that.*
— St. Teresa of Ávila

IF THE LOSS of our loved one wasn't bad enough, we frequently find that this person's death has triggered other losses. We may feel as if our family is falling apart because the person who held everyone together has died. With the death of our parents or our spouse, we may lose the family homestead. We may lose income or social status. We may lose our jobs or businesses that were jointly owned. We may have to sell some of our loved one's belongings or give them away.

Our self-esteem may suffer. We may feel as if we have lost our meaning or purpose in life because so much of our lives revolved around our loved one. These secondary losses make us feel as if everything in our world is unraveling. We feel as if we have to grieve each additional loss. We wonder if this cycle of loss will ever end. The answer is yes. The cycle will end, and we will reach a point in our lives where the acute pain associated with our losses ends.

If we think of the story of Noah and the ark, we can imagine that our grief is like the great flood that washed away everything on earth. Scripture tells us that the floodwaters remained for almost a year. When the waters finally dried up, Noah and his family came out of the ark and began a new life (Gn 7-8).

Grief over our losses will also come to an end, and we will one day begin a new stage in our lives.

PRAYER: *Lord, help me to deal with all of the losses that have come as a result of the death of my loved one. I am weary with grief. I feel as if the weight of these losses is almost too much to bear. I beg you to help me carry this load. Help me to see that there will be an end to this misery. Amen.*

❦❦❦❦❦

These words from the prophet Isaiah offer us the promise that God is all powerful and can give us the strength we need to get through the most difficult times in our lives:

> *Do you not know?*
> *Have you not heard?*
> *The LORD is God from of old,*
> *creator of the ends of the earth.*
> *He does not faint or grow weary,*
> *and his knowledge is beyond scrutiny.*
> *He gives power to the faint,*
> *abundant strength to the weak.*
> *Though young men faint and grow weary,*
> *and youths stagger and fall,*
> *They that hope in the LORD will renew their strength,*
> *they will soar on eagles' wings;*
> *They will run and not grow weary,*
> *walk and not grow faint. (Is 40:28-31)*

❦❦❦❦❦

27. ADVICE FROM OTHER PEOPLE

Everyone can master a grief but he that has it.
— WILLIAM SHAKESPEARE

WHEN WE'RE GRIEVING the death of a loved one, some people may give us bad advice. Their intentions are usually good, but the things they suggest are not always what we need to hear.

They may tell us not to cry, or not to think about the person, or to get on with our lives. What they don't realize is that we have to work through our grief, and that it takes a lot of effort and a lot of time.

Well-intentioned advice is often the opposite of what we really need or want to do. It's not uncommon for people to suggest that we get rid of our loved one's clothes and personal belongings as quickly as possible. What they don't realize is that keeping articles of clothing or mementoes of our loved one can actually help ease the pain of grief.

Sometimes, the things people say are shocking. They may tell us that God wanted our loved one more than we did or that we should be grateful that our loved one's illness is over.

Most people don't realize the inappropriateness of their comments or advice. It usually happens because they feel uncomfortable, and they don't know what to say. They rely on clichés and bits of useless information they may have heard. Grief is beyond their scope of understanding. They won't understand until they experience a significant loss in their own lives.

As upsetting as their comments may be, the best thing we can do is to just thank them for their concern, and then do what we know is the right thing for us to do.

PRAYER: *Lord, help me to be patient with people who don't understand the depths of my grief. Allow me to see the good intentions that lie beneath their comments. Bless all of us, and keep us in the healing warmth of your love. Amen.*

❦❦❦❦❦

The parents of St. Thérèse of Lisieux endured the death of three children in infancy and a fourth child who died at age five. Her mother later recalled the insensitive remarks made by well-meaning people:

> *When I closed the eyes of my dear little children and prepared them for burial, I was indeed grief-stricken.... People say to me: "It would have been much better if you had not given birth to those whom you lost so soon after their coming." I cannot bear to endure such sentiments! I do not find that the pains and sufferings can at all compare with the eternal happiness of my little ones, eternal happiness which, of course, would never have been theirs, had they never been born. Moreover, I have not lost them for always. Life is short. Soon I shall find my little ones in Heaven.*

❦❦❦❦❦

28. WHEN PEOPLE AVOID US

Misfortune shows those who are not really friends.
– ARISTOTLE

IT'S HARD TO DESCRIBE the feeling we get when we know that people are avoiding us. We see them on the street or in a store scurrying away so they don't have to talk to us. We see them at church trying not to make eye contact with us. We see them at school or at work pretending that they are too busy to chat. We see them at social events making excuses about having to talk to someone else so they don't have to talk to us.

Some of the people we thought were our friends stop calling, stop dropping by, or stop inviting us to do things with them.

Some of our friends will still talk to us about superficial things, but they will change the subject if we begin to talk about our loss. Some may even ask us how we are doing but then grow distant when we start to tell them how we really feel.

It creates a strange conflict inside us. Part of us wants to talk to these people. Another part of us is relieved that we don't have to talk to them.

The problem is that we live in a society that does not deal well with death. No one wants to talk about death. No one wants to think about it. No one wants it to happen to him or her.

When people avoid us, it is usually because they have never experienced a significant loss in their own lives. They don't know what to say to us. They don't feel comfortable even thinking about death. We become for them a grim reminder that death is

62

inevitable, and that someday they will also experience a loss.

Our only recourse when these things happen is to give these people to God and echo the words of Jesus on the cross: "Father, forgive them, they know not what they do" (Lk 23:34).

PRAYER: *Lord, you know how painful it is to be avoided by people you thought were your friends. I want to unite my pain with yours. I want to give you all of the people in my life who are avoiding me at this difficult time. I ask only that you will give me the grace to forgive them and to be there to help them when death touches their lives. Amen.*

❧❧❧❧❧

C. S. Lewis described the awkwardness of dealing with other people in this way: "An odd byproduct of my loss is that I'm aware of being an embarrassment to everyone I meet. At work, at the club, in the street, I see people, as they approach me, trying to make up their minds whether they'll 'say something about it' or not. I hate it if they do, and if they don't."

❧❧❧❧❧

29. The People Who Help

In everyone's life, at some time, our inner fire goes out.
It is then burst into flame by an encounter with another
human being. We should all be thankful for those people
who rekindle the inner spirit.
– ALBERT SCHWEITZER

WE ALL HAVE PEOPLE in our lives who help us through
our grief. Sometimes, we are surprised because the
people who help the most may not be our family
members or our closest friends. Sometimes, they are
people who have suffered a significant loss themselves.

When we think about the people who help us
the most, we often include those who are willing to
listen. They don't try to challenge us, or offer advice,
or push us in one direction or another. They just
listen. They allow us to talk about what happened.
They allow us to talk about our loved one. They allow us to talk about our own feelings of loss and
sorrow.

The people who help us the most include those
who do things for us without asking. They drop off
flowers or food, or help with household chores, or
run errands. We have many people who tell us, "Let
me know if you need anything." But the people who
really help are the ones who simply seem to know
what to do.

The best helpers are those who have their own
special way of making us feel better. They may not
do or say anything in particular. But their presence
seems to brighten our day. After being with them,
we feel as if our load is a little lighter. We feel as if we
have been given the strength to go on.

These people are instruments of God's love for us. The Holy Spirit works through them in powerful ways to comfort us, to calm us, and to help us deal with our sorrow and our pain.

PRAYER: *Lord, thank you for the people who have come into my life at this difficult time. I know that you are working through them. They give me comfort and strength. They are a sign to me of your loving presence in this world. Amen.*

❦❦❦❦

"When we honestly ask ourselves which persons in our lives mean the most to us, we often find that it is those who, instead of giving advice, solutions, or cures, have chosen rather to share our pain and touch our wounds with a warm and tender hand. The friend who can be silent with us in a moment of despair or confusion, who can stay with us in an hour of grief and bereavement, who can tolerate not knowing, not curing, not healing, and face with us the reality of our powerlessness, that is a friend who cares."
— *Henri Nouwen*

❦❦❦❦❦

30. DOING LITTLE THINGS

The person who moves a mountain begins
by carrying away small stones.
— CHINESE PROVERB

IT SOMETIMES FEELS as if grief is a mountain that looms before us. We have been told that we can't go over it and we can't go around it. We have to dig our own tunnel through the mountain.

The enormity of the task can seem overwhelming. We wonder how we can ever burrow our way through this mountain. The answer is that we work our way through the mountain by doing little things, step by step, stone by stone, one day at a time.

What kinds of little things can we do to chip away at this mountain of grief?

We can do all of those little things that we don't feel like doing when we are grieving. We can get up in the morning — even if we feel like staying in bed all day. We can do what we need to do for our own personal hygiene by making sure that our appearance is neat and clean.

We can do what we need to do to feed our bodies by eating regularly — whether we feel like eating or not. We can keep our homes tidy. We can do what we need to do for our families.

We can do what we need to do for our souls when we set aside time for prayer — even if we don't feel like praying.

Doing the little things that we need to do every day helps us chip away at the mountain of grief. It helps us establish a new routine. It helps us feel as if we are accomplishing something — even if it is just the minimum amount that we need to do for our daily survival.

Blessed Mother Teresa of Calcutta offers the following advice: "Be faithful in small things because it is in them that your strength lies."

PRAYER: *Lord, my grief is so profound that I don't want to do anything. Give me the strength to do the little things every day that are necessary for my life and the lives of those around me. Help me to see that by doing little things I am gradually working through this mountain of grief. Amen.*

St. Thérèse of Lisieux became a great saint — not by doing big things but by doing "little things with great love." People are attracted to the "little way" of St. Thérèse because it is a form of spirituality grounded in the ordinary that anyone can follow. Her "little way" was a personal commitment to offer to Jesus all of the tasks of everyday life. She saw each aspect of daily life as a gift. She understood that she had a choice about how she was going to live each minute of her life, and she chose to live it with love and to offer it to Jesus.

31. Visiting the Cemetery

When I am dead, come to me at my grave, and the more often the better. As you spoke to me when I was alive, do so now, for I am living, and I shall be forever.
— St. Seraphim of Sarov

For some of us, a visit to the cemetery is often a consolation, a time when we can sit quietly with our loved one, a time when we can talk and cry and share our feelings.

But some of us feel conflicted about visiting the cemetery. We may find that a visit to the cemetery is a painful memory, an uncomfortable reminder that our loved one is no longer with us. We may resist going to the cemetery, and we may feel guilty because we don't want to go. Or we may live far from the cemetery, and we simply cannot get there.

The reality is that there is no right or wrong when it comes to cemetery visits. If visiting the cemetery is not possible or makes us feel worse, then we shouldn't do it. If it's a comfort for us, then by all means, we should go as often as we want.

Father Ronald Rolheiser, O.M.I., described his visits to the graves of his parents as a good experience. "I feel some grounding in it, some deep rooting that helps center me. But this is not my real contact with them. No. I meet them among the living. I meet them when, in my own life, I live what was most distinctively them in terms of their love, faith, and virtue."

St. Monica emphasized to her sons that she was more concerned with having them pray for her than visit her grave. "Bury my body wherever you will; let not care of it cause you any concern," she told them. "One thing only I ask of you, that you remember me at the altar of the Lord wherever you may be."

Whether we like to go to the cemetery or not, it is important to remember that the cemetery is a holy place. The ground where our loved one lies has been blessed. So, whether our loved one is in a Catholic cemetery or in a grave or a mausoleum that has been individually blessed, we have the consolation of knowing that he or she is in a sacred space.

PRAYER: *Lord, I know that the body of my loved one has been laid to rest, but the soul of my loved one is now in your care. Have mercy on us all. Give me the courage to accept the death of my loved one with faith and hope that we shall one day be reunited. Amen.*

The early Christians venerated the final resting places of their loved ones in the catacombs and at their gravesites. In the Middle Ages, people began the practice of sprinkling graves with holy water. In modern times, we plant flowers or leave mementoes on graves. Blessed John Paul II reminds us that "prayer for the souls of the dead can be expressed in various ways, including a visit to the cemetery."

32. TEMPTATIONS

Let us ask our Lord to be with us in our moments of
temptation. We must not be afraid, because God
loves us and will not fail to help us.
— BLESSED MOTHER TERESA OF CALCUTTA

IT SEEMS UNFAIR that when we're grieving, we still
have to deal with temptations. But the reality is that
when we are in a weakened spiritual state, our temptations are often more frequent.

We may be tempted to be envious, if we start
to compare our lives to the lives of other people; or
to engage in self-pity, when we start to feel sorry for
ourselves; or to be prideful, when we refuse to allow
others to help us. We may be tempted to be bad tempered, when the pain of grief becomes our rationale
for not being nice to other people. Or we may find
ourselves criticizing others because we are so unhap-
py in our grief. Our greatest temptation may be to
despair, if we lose sight of God in our life.

Temptation is not a sin, but it can lead to sin. Our
response to temptation must always be an emphatic
"No! I am not going to give in to this!" When we re-
spond this way, we refuse to let the temptation linger
in our minds. We refuse to act on the temptation.

One of the best ways to overcome temptation
is to tell someone what is happening. St. Francis de
Sales tells us, "A temptation disclosed is a temptation half-vanquished." Whenever we feel as if we are
being battered with temptations, it is a good idea to
talk with a priest or spiritual adviser.

Prayer is another protection against temptation
because God will never refuse our request for aid.

Blessed Charles de Foucault assures us: "God, who knows with what clay he has formed us, and who loves us so much more than a mother could love her child, has told us, he who does not lie, that he would never turn away the one who comes to him."

The *Catechism of the Catholic Church* (CCC 2157) reminds us that making the Sign of the Cross strengthens us in times of temptation. Just repeating the name "Jesus" can chase temptations away.

St. Paul tells us that God does not cause temptations, but he allows temptations to occur and then offers us the graces we need to overcome those temptations. "God is faithful and will not let you be tried beyond your strength; but with the trial he will also provide a way out, so that you may be able to bear it" (1 Cor 10:13).

PRAYER: *Lord, I feel as if I am being battered with temptations. Protect me from these onslaughts. Help me to overcome my weaknesses. Give me the courage to move through this difficult time. Allow me to rely on you for assistance. Amen.*

❤❤❤❤❤

Temptation to despair may be connected to physical or chemical imbalances in our bodies. If we find ourselves slipping into a deep despair, with thoughts of ending our own lives, we must seek help immediately. Clinical depression is much more serious than the sadness we feel from our grief. It can be treated with the proper medication and therapy.

❤❤❤❤❤

71

33. Dealing With Doubts

"In my Father's house there are many dwelling places.
If there were not, would I have told you that I am going
to prepare a place for you?"
— John 14:2

WE WANT TO BELIEVE that our family members and
friends are with Jesus. We want to believe that we
will join them. But some of us may struggle with the
horrifying thought: *What if it isn't true?*

When this happens we enter into the same sea
of doubts that the apostles and Our Lady must have
experienced after the death of Jesus on Good Friday.
Did they recall that Jesus had told them that he was
going to prepare a place for them? Did they wonder
if it was true? We have one advantage that they did
not have. We know that on Easter Sunday Jesus rose
from the dead — and that after ascending into heav-
en, Jesus sent his Holy Spirit to be with them always.
Their grief was transformed into joy, and they spent
the rest of their lives spreading the Gospel message,
with the assurance that when they died, they would
be reunited with Jesus and with one another.

This is our Catholic faith. This is what we believe.
If doubts creep in, we have to remember that doubts
are not a denial of faith. Doubts invite us to a deeper
understanding of truth. Doubts force us to step out of
our grief and seek answers. We can talk to a priest or a
spiritual director about our doubts. We can ask faith-
filled friends how they dealt with doubts after a loved
one died. We can cry out to God, Our Lady, the saints,
or even the person we are grieving to help us.

During this time of doubts, our prayers echo the
words of the father in the Gospels, who had heard

that Jesus could heal people, and brought his son, with the hope that Jesus might heal him. The father wasn't sure Jesus could do it. He had doubts, but he was desperate, and so he pleaded with Jesus: "If you can do anything, have compassion on us and help us" (Mk 9:22). When Jesus assured him that "everything is possible to one who has faith," the father replied, "I do believe, help my unbelief!" (Mk 9:23, 24).

Jesus cured the boy, and the father's doubts turned into deep faith. Our doubts can also deepen our faith. But first we have to admit that we are struggling. We have to seek God's help. It is only then that the light of truth will filter into our darkness.

PRAYER: *Lord, I believe, but like the father in the Gospels, I need help with my unbelief. Guide me to someone that I can talk with about these dark feelings. Give me the courage to be open about my doubts. Help me to find comfort in your assurance that when I die, a place for me has been prepared by you, and that my loved ones will be waiting to greet me. Amen.*

❦❦❦❦❦

In halting words, a grief-stricken St. Elizabeth Ann Seton described her doubts about seeing her daughter again, and the spiritual consolation that followed when she realized that God was with her in her grief:

> *On the grave of [Nina] — begging crying to Mary to behold her son and plead for us, and to Jesus to behold his Mother — to pity a mother — a poor, poor mother — so uncertain of a reunion — then the Soul quieted even by the desolation of the falling leaves around began to cry out from eternity to eternity thou art God — all shall perish and pass away — but thou remainest forever.*

❦❦❦❦❦

34. Giving Up Control

"Do not let your hearts be troubled. You have faith in God; have faith also in me."
— John 14:1

We tend to operate under the illusion that we are in control. The death of a loved one shatters that illusion. Grief pushes us out of our normal lives and into lives that are filled with uncertainty. It turns our world upside down. It brings us face-to-face with our own vulnerability. It forces us to admit that we do not know what tomorrow will bring.

We may try to continue the illusion that we are under control, but we find ourselves getting frustrated time and time again. Grief is too unpredictable. We don't know from one minute to the next whether we will be up or down. It's much easier if we give up the illusion that we are in control and allow ourselves to move through our grief, taking each day as it comes.

Giving up control does not mean that we don't continue with our normal responsibilities in life. It means that we empty ourselves of all the things in our life that are not important. We accept that things will not always go the way we planned. We stop trying to do everything ourselves and ask other people to help us. We surrender our dreams for the future that won't come true, and we learn to appreciate the present moment. We refuse to worry, and we accept that whatever is going to happen will happen, whether we worry about it or not.

Giving up control is an important element in the grieving process. When we empty ourselves of things that are not really important, we make room for God to fill the empty spaces of our being. It's a process of placing our trust in God. We have to believe that God will carry us through this difficult time. We have to place God in control of our life. We have to heed the words of Scripture: "Trust in the LORD with all your heart, / on your own intelligence do not rely; / In all your ways be mindful of him, / and he will make straight your paths" (Prv 3:5-6).

PRAYER: *Lord, my whole world is falling apart. Everything seems to be spinning out of control. The harder I try to regain control, the worse it gets. So I surrender it all to you. I give you control of my life. I trust that you will carry me through this time of turmoil. Lord, help me. Amen.*

There's an old story about how they used to catch monkeys in Africa. The people from the village would put peanuts in the bottom of a long-necked jar. The jars were placed by the side of the river. The monkeys would come to the river and reach into the jar to grab the peanuts. It was impossible, however, for the monkeys to remove their hands from the jars because the peanuts were held tightly in their fists. As the monkeys struggled with the jars, the villagers would sneak up from behind and capture them. The monkeys lost their lives because they refused to open their hands and let go of the peanuts.

❦❦❦❦❦

35. Lighting Candles

Jesus spoke to them again, saying, "I am the light of the world. Whoever follows me will not walk in darkness, but will have the light of life."
— John 8:12

MANY OF US FIND comfort in lighting candles in memory of our loved ones. Since the earliest days of Christianity, candles have symbolized the pure light of Christ that pierces the darkness, overcomes evil, and offers hope to the world.

We know that the early Christians burned candles at the burial places of the martyrs in the catacombs. The light of the candle burned as a silent vigil in remembrance of the person. The word *vigil* comes from the Latin word that means waiting or watching. When we light vigil candles for our loved ones, we wait and watch until we can be reunited with them.

Throughout the Middle Ages and into the present day, people also lit vigil, or votive, candles in church or in front of a saintly image as a way to ask for favors or intercession. When we light votive candles for our loved ones, we pray for the repose of their souls. We can also light a votive candle when we ask our loved ones to pray for our intentions.

In addition, we can light a candle in the privacy of our own home as a simple remembrance of our loved ones. Watching the flickering of the flame, smelling the scent of the wax, and allowing ourselves to be united in prayer with our loved ones often gives us a sense of peace that we cannot find in other forms of prayer.

Lighting a candle also reminds us that "God is light, and in him there is no darkness" (1 Jn 1:5). We can allow the light of the candle to become a sign to us that the darkness of our own bereavement will eventually end.

PRAYER: *Lord, I light a candle in memory of my loved ones. May the light from the flickering flame break through the darkness of my grief and allow me to see more clearly your loving kindness and mercy. May the light from the candle assure me that my prayers for my loved ones and me are reaching you in heaven. Amen.*

In the Jewish faith, family members light a Yahrzeit candle during their time of mourning. The Yahrzeit candle is lit again on the eve of the anniversary of the person's death and burns for twenty-four hours in that person's memory. The candle is lit at home or at the gravesite. The custom developed from the words in the Book of Proverbs: "A lamp from the LORD is human life-breath" (Prv 20:27).

36. Where Did They Go?

*The souls of the righteous are in the hand of God, / and
no torment shall touch them.*
— Wisdom 3:1

ONE OF THE MOST DIFFICULT questions that we face
when a loved one dies is this: Where is that person
now? We want our loved one to come back just for
an instant so that we know everything is all right.

There is an old Eskimo legend that says the stars
are "openings in the heaven where the love of our
lost ones pours through and shines down upon us
to let us know they are happy."

Some of us may have had an experience after
the death of a loved one that we interpret as a sign. It
might be something unusual that happens. It might
be a dream. It might be a sense that the person is
present, even though he or she cannot be seen. It
might be an experience that simply cannot be put
into words, but which leaves us with the assurance
that there is life after death.

Sometimes our greatest fear is that our deceased
family members or friends are in purgatory. It helps
if we think of purgatory, not as a place of suffering,
but as a place where souls prepare for total union
with God. St. Catherine of Genoa assures us that
souls in purgatory experience more peace and happiness than they did on earth because they know
they are on their way to heaven. Blessed John Paul
II describes purgatory as the place where every trace
of sin is washed away and every imperfection in our
souls is healed. St. John of the Cross tells us that
once we shed our worldliness, we will enter into a
perfect union of love with God.

St. Paul promises that union with God will be more wonderful than we could ever imagine: " 'What eye has not seen, and ear has not heard, / and what has not entered the human heart, / what God has prepared for those who love him,' this God has revealed to us through the Spirit" (1 Cor 2:9-10).

When we find ourselves wondering where our loved ones are, we need to calm our fears with the assurance that our loved ones are in the hands of God, and that someday we will join them. St. Cyril of Jerusalem tells us: "The Lord is very loving toward human beings. He is quick to pardon, but slow to punish. Therefore, no one should ever despair of salvation."

PRAYER: *Lord, I am fearful about my loved ones. Calm my fears. Help me to transform my fear into prayer for my loved ones. Allow me to intercede on their behalf so that they may enter into your glorious presence and be with you for all eternity. Amen.*

❧❧❧❧❧

When we are worried about our loved ones, we can turn to these comforting words in the Book of Wisdom for hope and consolation:

> *They seemed, in the view of the foolish, to be dead;*
> *and their passing away was thought an affliction*
> *and their going forth from us, utter destruction.*
> *But they are in peace.*
> *For if to others, indeed, they seem punished,*
> *yet is their hope full of immortality;*
> *Chastised a little, they shall be greatly blessed,*
> *because God tried them*
> *and found them worthy of himself. (Wis 3:2-5)*

❧❧❧❧❧

37. THE COMMUNION OF SAINTS

We believe in the communion of all the faithful of Christ,
those who are pilgrims on earth, the dead who are
being purified, and the blessed in heaven, all together
forming one Church; and we believe that in this
communion, the merciful love of God and his saints
is always [attentive] to our prayers.
— POPE PAUL VI (AS CITED IN CCC 96)

ONE OF THE MOST CONSOLING elements of faith when we are grieving the loss of a loved one is our belief in the Communion of Saints. From the earliest days of the Church, Catholics have believed that when people die, their time on earth ends, but their lives continue with God. We believe that there is a spiritual union between the souls on earth, the souls in purgatory, and the souls in heaven. We call this the Communion of Saints because it binds us all together in the mystical body of Christ.

Because we are all part of the Communion of Saints, we can pray for one another, intercede for one another, and maintain the bonds of love we have with one another. Blessed Mother Teresa explained it this way: "My mother and sister must be very happy to be home with God, and I am sure their love and prayers are always with me. When I go home to God, for death is nothing else but going home to God, the bond of love will be unbroken for all eternity."

Our belief in the Communion of Saints offers us comfort. We can pray for our loved ones, and we can be assured that they are praying for us. We can know that love never dies, and that we will one day be united in the love of God.

PRAYER: *Lord, I believe in the Communion of Saints. I believe that I am with you, and that my loved one is with you. I believe that we are spiritually united in the bond of your love. Accept my humble prayers for my loved one. Keep me open to the intercessions that my loved one is making on my behalf. Bless all of us, and help us to carry on. Amen.*

❦❦❦❦❦

Father Bede Jarrett, O.P., offers this consoling prayer that helps us to better understand the Communion of Saints:

We give them back to you, O God, who gave them to us. Yet as you did not lose them in the giving, so we do not lose them by their return. Not as the world gives do you give, O lover of souls. What you give, you do not take away, for what is yours is ours also if we are yours. And life is eternal and love is immortal, and death is only a horizon, and a horizon is nothing save the limit of our sight. Lift us up, strong Son of God, that we may see further; cleanse our eyes that we may see more clearly; draw us closer to yourself that we may know ourselves to be nearer to our loved ones who are with you. And while you prepare a place for us, prepare us also for that happy place, that where you are we may also be for evermore.

❦❦❦❦❦

38. Praying for Our Loved Ones

*We have loved him during life, let us not abandon
him, until we have conducted him by our prayers
into the house of the Lord.*
— St. Ambrose

FOR MANY OF US, praying for our departed loved ones
is a great consolation. It gives us the feeling that we're
doing something. It helps us to still feel connected. It
helps us to cope with our fears, our loneliness, and
our pain. Praying for the dead is a tradition that has
been passed down through the centuries by people
of all faiths. Prayer helps us through our grief. It is a
powerful way to keep our love for this person alive.

We know that prayer was important for the early Christians. A second-century tomb of one early
Christian is inscribed with the words: "Let every
friend who observes this pray for me." Other mark-
ings on the walls of the catacombs contain prayers
such as "Peace be with you," "May God refresh your
soul," and "May you live among the saints."

We have many ways to pray for our loved ones.
We can have Masses celebrated for them. We can
create a perpetual remembrance by enrolling them
with a religious community that will include them
in daily prayers. We can pray novenas for the dead.
We can place them in the hands of Our Lady of Sor-
rows by praying the Rosary. We can pray for them in
a special way on All Souls' Day and throughout the
month of November. Some parishes have a Book of
the Dead, where we can inscribe their names. We
can pray the traditional prayer: "Eternal rest grant
unto them, O Lord, and let perpetual light shine

upon them. May their souls and all the souls of the faithful departed, through the mercy of God, rest in peace. Amen."

We can also pray spontaneously for our loved ones by simply saying, "Lord, have mercy." We can pray by offering up the pain of our grief for our loved ones. We can ask the Lord to accept our groaning, our sighs, and our tears as a prayer for our loved ones.

The best way to pray for our loved ones is at Mass. It unites us and our loved ones in the healing power of the Eucharist.

PRAYER: *Lord, I am offering you the pain of my grief as a prayer for my loved one. Unite us in your saving love. Give us the graces that we both need in order to draw closer to you. Amen.*

❅❅❅❅❅

St. Ignatius of Loyola wrote this beautiful prayer for people who have died: "Receive, Lord, in tranquility and peace, the souls of your servants who have departed out of this present life to be with you. Give them the life that knows no age, the good things that do not pass away, through Jesus Christ, Our Lord."

❅❅❅❅❅

39. Problems With Prayer

God says, "When you are dry, empty, sick, or weak, at
such a time is your prayer most pleasing to Me, even
though you find little enough to enjoy in it."
— Julian of Norwich

Prayer is sometimes difficult when we are grieving.
We may start off with good intentions to pray but
end up distracted, with our minds flitting from one
thing to another. We may think there should be
some special feeling when we pray, but it is not unusual for a grieving person to feel nothing, or worse,
to feel a sense of revulsion at the idea of prayer.

We may feel guilty because we know that we
should pray, but our minds, our bodies, and our
souls feel numb. Our lack of desire to pray may
include not wanting to go to Mass. It may be too
painful to go back into the church where the funeral
was held. We may be embarrassed because we cry
when we hear certain hymns. We may not want to
be around other people.

All of these are normal spiritual responses when
we are grieving. We need to remind ourselves that
authentic prayer is simply an attempt to place ourselves in the presence of God. St. Francis de Sales
offers the following advice: "When you come before
the Lord, talk to him if you can; if you can't, just stay
there, let yourself be seen, and don't try too hard to
do anything else."

Our prayer is not a success or failure because of
our ability to concentrate or how we feel at any given
moment. The only thing we have to do is to come

to the Lord in our pain and in our grief. We can let God do the rest for us.

St. Teresa of Ávila assures us: "One must not think that a person who is suffering is not praying. He is offering up his sufferings to God, and many a time he is praying much more truly than one who goes away by himself and meditates his head off, and, if he has squeezed out a few tears, thinks that is prayer."

So we shouldn't feel discouraged if we have difficulty praying. The Lord understands.

PRAYER: *Lord, I am distracted and discouraged. I feel as if I can't pray. Allow me to simply sit here in your presence with the hope that you will comfort me in my distress. Strengthen my faith so that I can truly believe that you are with me in my grief. Help me to believe that the pain of my grief is part of my prayer. Amen.*

St. Thérèse of Lisieux offers good advice for those who find it difficult to pray: "Sometimes, when I find myself spiritually in dryness so great that I cannot produce a single good thought, I recite very slowly an Our Father or a Hail Mary. These prayers alone console me. They nourish my soul."

✦✦✦✦✦

40. TRYING TO UNDERSTAND

Pain in itself is not unbearable; it is the failure to understand its meaning that is unbearable.
– VENERABLE FULTON SHEEN

ONE OF THE MOST DIFFICULT aspects of grief is trying to find meaning in our pain. St. Paul tells us that "all things work for good for those who love God" (Rom 8:28).

We want to believe that something good will come from the death of our loved one, but our vision is blinded by our sorrow. We can't see beyond the immense pain that we are feeling today, and our inability to understand makes everything worse.

We are like the apostles after the death of Jesus. They had given up three years of their lives to follow Jesus. All of their hopes and dreams were destroyed when Jesus died. They feared that their own lives might be in danger. They did not understand. Even after Jesus rose from the dead, they could not comprehend the immensity of what had happened. It wasn't until the Holy Spirit descended upon them on Pentecost that they discovered the meaning and purpose in everything that had happened. It took their lives in an entirely different direction.

We will also find meaning in the death of our loved one. Like the apostles, we will find it hard to understand in the beginning. But in time, we will develop a deeper understanding of ourselves and our loved one because of our grief. We may discover new insights. We may see new opportunities to help others because of what happened to us. We may find a new outlook on life and a new way of living.

Like the grain of wheat that Jesus talks about in the Gospels, our old life died with the death of our loved one, but a new life for us will begin again, and our new life will bear good fruit (Jn 12:24).

PRAYER: *Lord, I don't understand. I am consumed with grief. But I believe in your promise of new life. I believe that when I emerge from this time of bereavement, I will still miss my loved one, but I will begin to see deeper meaning and purpose in my life. Help me, Lord. Give me the courage to move through my grief. Amen.*

❦❦❦❦❦

Erma Bombeck offers us these comforting words of wisdom: "The longer I live, the more convinced I become that surviving changes us. After the bitterness, the anger, the guilt, and the despair are tempered by time, we look at life differently."

❦❦❦❦❦

41. LETTING GO

I know why we try to keep the dead alive: we try to
keep them alive in order to keep them with us.
I also know that if we are to live ourselves there
comes a point at which we must relinquish
the dead, let them go, keep them dead.
— JOAN DIDION

AN IMPORTANT PART of our grieving process is the gradual letting go of our loved ones. We have to accept their deaths and let them go if we want to move on with our lives.

On a rational level, we know that our loved ones are no longer living. But on an emotional level, we don't want to accept that reality. We are torn apart inside ourselves. So we cling to our loved ones because we don't want to let them go.

In many ways, we are like Mary Magdalene, who tried to cling to the Risen Christ on Easter Sunday morning. But Jesus told her, "Stop holding on to me, for I have not yet ascended to the Father" (Jn 20:17).

When we refuse to let go of our loved ones, we become frozen in time. We enter into a kind of living death, cutting ourselves off from people around us, and refusing to allow our lives to continue.

At some point on our grief journey, we will come to the understanding that we have to let our loved ones go. Letting go does not mean that we don't care about them anymore. Letting go does not mean that we forget about them.

Letting go means that we are willing to move forward in our own lives without the presence of our loved ones. Letting go brings us to a place where we feel the pain of our loss, but at the same time we recognize and appreciate that we grieve deeply because we loved deeply. Our loss is significant, but we can be grateful for the time that we had with them, and we can go on with our lives because we know this is what our loved ones would want us to do.

PRAYER: *Lord, I am like Mary Magdalene. I want to cling to my loved ones. Give me the courage to stop clinging and let my loved ones go. Help me to understand that letting go means that I will place my loved ones in your loving care. Amen.*

❤❤❤❤❤

After the death of his father, St. Gregory Nazianzen, who lived in the fourth century, offered the following words of comfort to his grief-stricken mother: "Does the thought of separation grieve you? Then let hope cheer you.... Great is the loss we have suffered, for great was the blessing we enjoyed."

❤❤❤❤❤

42. THE RESURRECTION OF THE BODY

I believe in ... the resurrection of the body
and life everlasting.
– THE APOSTLES' CREED

ONE OF THE GREATEST COMFORTS in our grief is the belief that Jesus will return again at the end of the world, and that the bodies of the dead will be resurrected in the same way that Jesus was resurrected on the first Easter.

But sometimes we wonder what will happen. How will we look? Will we be young or old? Will our loved ones know us? Will we know them? Will we remember what our lives on earth together were like?

In St. John's first letter, he tells us: "Beloved, we are God's children now; what we shall be has not yet been revealed. We do know that when it is revealed we shall be like him, for we shall see him as he is" (1 Jn 3:2-3).

We know from Scripture accounts that when Jesus rose from the dead, his body was glorified. At first, Mary Magdalene did not recognize him; but as soon as he said her name, she knew instantly that it was Jesus.

We know that Jesus was able to pass through locked doors. We know that he was able to eat. We know that the wounds from his crucifixion remained, but that he did not appear to be in pain. He told the disciples: "Look at my hands and my feet, that it is I myself. Touch me and see, because a ghost does not have flesh and bones as you can see I have" (Lk 24:39).

St. Paul tells us that our bodies will decay when we are buried, but when we are raised our bodies will be incorruptible. "It is sown weak; it is raised powerful. It is sown a natural body; it is raised a spiritual body" (1 Cor 15:43-44).

We know that the Risen Christ ascended into heaven with the promise that he would one day return. We cling to that promise. When we die, we hope that we will be united with Jesus and with our loved ones forever in eternity.

PRAYER: *Lord, I believe that you died and rose again. I believe that you ascended into heaven. I believe that you will come again. I believe that my loved ones and I will also be resurrected, and that we will be united with you forever. Give me the courage to move through the remaining days of my life with this steadfast faith. Amen.*

These words of Jesus before he died challenge us to affirm our belief in the resurrection of the body and eternal life: "I am the resurrection and the life; whoever believes in me, even if he dies, will live, and everyone who lives and believes in me will never die. Do you believe this?" (Jn 11:25-26).

43. The Gift of Laughter

*How lovely is the sun after rain, and how
lovely is laughter after sorrow.*
— Tunisian proverb

It may sound strange, but laughter is like the silver lining in the dark cloud of grief. A part of us may find it incomprehensible that we could laugh when our pain is so intense. Some of us may feel guilty if we find ourselves laughing in the midst of our grief.

But laughter is just as much a gift for us as tears. There is nothing wrong with laughter. It was part of our lived experience with our loved one, and now it needs to be incorporated into our memories of that person. Laughter is simply another indication of how much we loved and appreciated that person. We may even find ourselves laughing and crying at the same time.

Laughter releases pent-up emotions. It increases endorphins, which make us feel better. It relaxes us. It lowers blood pressure. It elevates the level of oxygen in the blood. It strengthens the immune system.

Sharing happy memories and funny stories about our loved one helps us in our grief. We can say to family members and friends, "Do you remember when ..." We can ask others to recall their lighthearted moments with our loved one. It triggers a deeper level of sharing that makes everyone feel better.

Laughing at ourselves is another healthy way to deal with grief. If we can laugh at some of the mistakes we make, at our memory lapses, and at our feeble attempts to do something that we simply cannot do, we take some of the sting out of our grief.

Laughter makes us feel better — even if it's only for a few brief moments. So let's thank God for the gift of laughter, which gives us a brief respite from our grief and helps us to continue on our journey.

PRAYER: *Lord, I don't feel like laughing, and when I do laugh, I feel as if I am in some way betraying my loved one. Help me to laugh. Lighten my heart. Instill in me a sense of joy. Let me feel so much gratitude for the good times I shared with my loved one that I can laugh out loud in thanksgiving. Amen.*

❦❦❦❦❦

Laughter is such a healing part of the grieving process that bereavement counselors suggest that grieving people set aside time every day for laughter. You might decide to watch a funny movie or television program. You might want to read the comics or a funny book. You might want to think about something your loved one always did to make you laugh. Don't be surprised if your laughter is mixed with tears. You will get the benefits of both.

If you don't find humor in any of these options, some counselors recommend that you sit down, once a day, and simply try to laugh out loud. Forcing yourself to laugh for thirty seconds can produce the same good effects as spontaneous laughter.

So find a way to laugh. Laugh in memory of the good times you shared with your loved one. Laugh because your loved one would not want you to be sad forever. Laugh because it's good for you!

❦❦❦❦❦

44. Grief Surges

*There are moments, most unexpectedly, when something
inside me tries to assure me that I don't really mind
so much, not so very much, after all.... Then comes a
sudden jab of red-hot memory and all this "commonsense"
vanishes like an ant in the mouth of a furnace.*
— C. S. Lewis

GRIEVING IS LIKE A ROLLER COASTER. One day we may
actually feel good, and the next day something unexpected can bring back the raw intensity of the pain.
These experiences are called "grief surges," and they
happen without warning.

Someone says something, or we hear a song, or
a memory pops into our minds, or we smell a familiar scent, or we see someone or something that
reminds us of our loved one, and the pain comes
back with a power that can take our breath away.
All of the time that we have spent grieving seems to
slip away, and we are plunged back into the depths
of our pain.

There is no way to prepare for a grief surge because we never know when one will happen. They
tend to occur more and with greater intensity in the
first year. As time goes on, we find that they become
less frequent, but they can still occur many years
later.

When it happens, we may feel upset or embarrassed. We may start to cry. But that is all right. The
best way to deal with a grief surge is to simply let the
pain wash over us like a wave in the ocean. We feel
the pain, and then allow it to ebb away.

PRAYER: *Lord, I feel as if I am on an emotional roller coaster as I grieve the loss of my loved one. Help me to feel grateful for the good days. Strengthen me in the difficult moments. Allow me to see that you are always with me in good times and in bad. Amen.*

❦❦❦❦❦

C. S. Lewis described a grief surge in this way: "Tonight all the hells of young grief have opened again; the mad words, the bitter resentment, the fluttering in the stomach, the nightmare unreality, the wallowed-in tears. For in grief nothing 'stays put.' One keeps on emerging from a phase, but it always recurs."

❦❦❦❦❦

45. Grieving Together

Shared sorrow is half a sorrow.
— Swedish proverb

Grief is always more complicated when it affects a number of people who are all devastated by the loss of a loved one. But there are some things that we can do to help and encourage one another on our shared journey through grief.

We can begin by accepting that different people in the family will grieve in different ways. Some may want to talk or cry together. Others may be more private in their grief. Some family members may turn to friends outside the family for comfort and support. We have to let them go. Likewise, we may find that we need the help of a counselor or support group to deal with our own grief.

We should never try to force someone to grieve in a specific way. We can assure family members that there is no right or wrong way to grieve. It is all very personal and unique.

It is important, however, to try to keep the lines of communication open. We can say, "I'm not having a very good day today." We can ask, "How are you doing with your grief?" We can invite, "I'm going to the cemetery if you would like to come along." We can affirm, "This is difficult for all of us. Is there something I can do to help you?"

A major part of grieving together is talking about how we will deal with family responsibilities that were held by the person who died. We also have to deal with deciding how we will distribute precious keepsakes and possessions.

We have to be careful about our own expectations for family members and their expectations for us. We may want things from them that they cannot give. Likewise, they may want things from us that we are unable or unwilling to do. Sometimes, it may mean that we have to bring in another person to help us sort things out.

Last but not least, we have to always keep in mind that the one thing we share is our love for the person who has died and our love for one another. We have to believe that no matter what happens, love will carry us through this difficult time.

PRAYER: *Lord, I see the people around me struggling with their own grief. I don't always know what to do. I don't always say the right thing. Allow me to place these people in your arms. I pray that you will comfort them in their sorrow. I pray also that you will guide me in ways that can help them through their grief. Amen.*

❖❖❖❖❖

St. Paul offers these comforting words:

> Blessed be the God and Father of our Lord Jesus Christ, the Father of compassion and God of all encouragement, who encourages us in our every affliction, so that we may be able to encourage those who are in any affliction with the encouragement with which we ourselves are encouraged by God.
> (2 Cor 1:3-4)

❖❖❖❖❖

46. Dreading Special Days

*I have learned to live each day as it comes, and not
to borrow trouble by dreading tomorrow. It is the dark
menace of the future that makes cowards of us.*
— Dorothy Day

Throughout the first year of our bereavement,
we are tormented with dread over how we will get
through birthdays, anniversaries, holidays, and other
special occasions. As each special event approaches,
the raw pain of grief returns. We think about what
we were doing last year. Our sadness intensifies. We
don't feel like celebrating. We wish that we could flip
the calendar so that we don't have to go through this
special day. Other people try to assure us that it will
be all right — and on one level we know that they are
right, but on another level we don't believe them.

Our greatest temptation is to isolate ourselves
and allow the day to pass by alone. But often, because
of children and other family members, we can't escape. We know that we will have to take part in the
celebrations. We will have to go through the motions.

What we quickly learn, however, is that our fears
about getting through the day are much worse than
the day itself. If we are able to share memories of our
loved one, the day turns out to be better than we an-
ticipated. For some of us, doing something completely different on the special day, such as serving meals
at a soup kitchen or volunteering to help people who
are less fortunate, alleviates the pain. We can also ease
our grief by planning to do something special for family members and friends. We can use the special day
as a time when we give some of our loved one's prized
personal possessions to family members and friends.

Placing a spiritual emphasis on the day also helps. We can arrange for a Mass to be celebrated. We can make a donation to a favorite charity. We can set aside quiet time for prayer.

There is no question that these special days are difficult. But we can (and we will) get through them.

PRAYER: *Lord, you know how much I am dreading the next special event without the presence of my loved one. Calm my fears. Give me the inspiration I need to plan something positive and meaningful for this day. Give me the courage to move through the day. Amen.*

❦❦❦❦❦

Here are some things that can help as we approach holidays and other special events:

- ❦ *Talk about your fears. Tell family members and friends that you are anxious about what the upcoming day will bring.*
- ❦ *Plan ahead for what you will do on that day.*
- ❦ *If you are expected to be at a celebration, decide ahead of time how long you will stay, and let everyone know your plans. You can always change your mind and stay longer.*
- ❦ *Give yourself permission to cry.*
- ❦ *Think about starting new family traditions that will honor the memory of your loved one.*
- ❦ *Eliminate any old traditions that are too painful or too much work.*
- ❦ *Put a photo of your loved one in a prominent place or light a memorial candle to recognize that even though this person is no longer here physically, the love and spirit of the person remain alive in the hearts of all who grieve the loss.*

❦❦❦❦❦

47. Looking at a Bigger Picture

*Do not measure your loss by itself; if you do, it will
seem intolerable; but if you will take all human
affairs into account you will find that some
comfort is to be derived from them.*
— St. Basil

GRIEF IMPOSES a kind of tunnel vision. We find it
hard to see beyond our own pain. When we look
around us, we can't understand how everything in
the world continues to go on as normal when we
have suffered such a devastating loss. We see people
smiling and laughing. We see people coming and going, busy with their lives, and completely oblivious
to our pain.

We may acknowledge that we once lived in
a carefree world. We loved our lives. We looked
forward to the future with the anticipation that
good things would continue to happen. But those
memories only seem to make our loss even more
unbearable.

It may be hard for us to believe that one of the
best ways to break through our pain is to find other
people who are also grieving. When we connect with
other grieving people, we quickly discover that their
stories become "our" story, and the sense of solidar-
ity makes us feel better.

We discover that other people feel some of the
same feelings that we feel. We discover that other people have found coping mechanisms that can help us.
We are no longer alone in our grief. We are part of a
bigger picture. We begin to believe that if other people
can get through their grief, we can get through ours.

Sometimes, in sharing our stories, we also begin to see how God is working in our lives. We recognize that in the midst of sorrow and loss, we gain new insights about life, about ourselves, and about God.

We become more understanding. We become more compassionate. We become less self-centered. We begin to see that there is more to life than our grief. We begin to believe that we will survive. As Helen Keller once said, "Although the world is full of suffering, it is full also of overcoming it."

PRAYER: *Lord, I am having a hard time seeing beyond my own grief. Help me to see a bigger picture. Help me to reach out to other people. And in hearing their stories, allow me to see you working in their lives. Amen.*

❈❈❈❈❈

There is an old story about a man who had been asked by God to push a large rock. So the man started to push the rock, but it wouldn't move. The man continued to push, but after a while he began to feel discouraged. Finally, God spoke to the man, reminding him that he had never asked him to move the rock, only to push it. And then God pointed out all the good things that had happened to the man while he pushed: his muscles had become strong, and the man was pleasing to God because he was doing God's will.

When the man viewed the task from a human perspective, he felt that it was useless. When he saw the task from God's perspective, he realized that there was meaning and purpose in what he was doing. He just couldn't see it from his own narrow perspective.

❈❈❈❈❈

48. GRATITUDE

Say not in grief, "He is no more," but live
in thankfulness that he was.
— HEBREW PROVERB

WE ARE SOMETIMES SURPRISED to discover that gratitude is one of the best ways to deal with our grief.
But feelings of gratitude do not happen automatical-
ly. We have to consciously think about those things
in our own lives and in the lives of our loved ones
that make us feel thankful.

We may be grateful for the time we had together. We may be grateful that our loved one is no
longer suffering. We may be grateful for treasured
memories. We may be grateful for advice that our
loved one gave us. We may be grateful for something
that our loved one left us.

Maybe we're grateful for something that we
didn't know about our loved one until after he or
she died. Maybe we're grateful for something that we
discovered about ourselves.

We may be grateful for all of the small acts of
kindness from the people in our lives, especially
those who are helping us through our grief. Maybe
we're grateful because someone shared with us a
memory of our loved one. Maybe we're grateful because someone did something special for us.

We can be grateful for those little distractions
in life that give us a short reprieve from the pain
of our grief. We can be grateful for a sunny day, a
rainbow, the warmth of the sun, or a cooling breeze.
We can be grateful for the smile of a stranger or the
gift of a good friend. We can be grateful for what we

are learning about ourselves because of this painful experience.

Feeling grateful does not mean that we don't feel our loss. Our loss is real. Gratitude is simply the other side of the coin. It offsets our loss by allowing us to appreciate the good things connected to our loved one and to the other people around us.

Gratitude also helps us to offset anxiety. It quells our feelings of loneliness and insecurity. It alleviates stress. It softens our feelings of sadness. It banishes feelings of envy. It keeps us from taking our lives for granted. Gratitude is a gift that we give to ourselves.

PRAYER: *Lord, instill in me a sense of gratitude for all the good things that my loved one brought into my life. Help me to be thankful for all of the people who are helping me through this difficult time. Give me the ability to see the good things that are happening all around me. Amen.*

Robert Louis Stevenson created this beautiful image of gratitude in Prayers Written at Vailima: *"And now, when the clouds gather and the rain impends over the forest and our house, permit us not to be cast down; let us not lose the savor of past mercies and past pleasures; but, like the voice of a bird singing in the rain, let grateful memory survive in the hour of darkness."*

49. HOPE

*For you will surely have a future, / and your
hope will not be cut off.*
— PROVERBS 23:18

UNTIL WE'VE SUFFERED a significant loss, we don't really understanding the words of St. Paul warning us not to grieve like those "who have no hope" (1 Thes 4:13).

It is only when we have experienced the pain of losing a loved one that we realize how grief can take us into a dark place, where we feel as if we are completely lost. Hope is what keeps us afloat in our sea of misery.

The dictionary tells us that "hope" is our ability to desire, to anticipate, to expect with confidence. St. Paul tells us that real hope comes from our belief that the Lord Jesus has died and is risen from the dead (1 Thes 4:14).

Pope Benedict XVI expands on this definition of "hope" in his encyclical *Spe Salvi* (on Christian hope) when he tells us that hope means knowing Jesus Christ. It means knowing that "I am definitively loved and whatever happens to me — I am awaited by this Love" (*Spe Salvi*, n. 3).

Hope instills in us the promise that we will see our loved one again. Hope gives us the assurance that we will be together again for all eternity.

Hope does not take away our sadness. It does not lessen our pain. But it does give something to hold on to in our grief. Hope keeps us from slipping into self-pity and despair. It helps us to understand the words of the prophet Baruch: "With mourning and lament I sent you away, / but God will give you back to me / with gladness and joy forever" (Bar 4:23).

There is a certain consolation that comes with the hope of some day being united with our loved one. We know that God is love. We know that love never dies. We know that we loved the person who died. We know that this person loved us. We know that we are both loved by God.

So we move through our grief, holding on to the hope that one day God will wipe every tear from our eyes and "there shall be no more death or mourning, wailing or pain" (Rev 21:4).

PRAYER: *Lord, strengthen my hope. Help me to live each day with the hope of being united with you and with my loved one who has died. Give me the courage to move on through my grief. Help me to believe that you will save me and heal me. Amen.*

❦❦❦❦❦

After the death of his wife, St. Francis Borgia clung to hope in the midst of his grief when he wrote:

> *Our Lord has willed to call back to himself the duchess whose death leaves this house so dejected and tearful as anyone can think. By the mercy of Our Lord God, however, her life was spent so much in His service, and the end of her life was so Christian, that we are left with good reason to believe that her soul is in heaven by the merits of Jesus' most precious blood.*

❦❦❦❦❦

50. Healing

*Time heals grief ... for we change and are
no longer the same person.*
— Blaise Pascal

THE GRIEVING PROCESS is different for everyone, but most of us discover that by the end of the first year the raw pain and the deep sorrow begin to lessen. We realize that we are beginning to heal. We still miss our loved one, but the edges of our grief are not as ragged.

We begin to feel better physically. Our eating and sleeping habits stabilize. Our energy returns. We don't cry as much. We don't sigh as much. Our breathing patterns return to normal.

We no longer feel as if we are going crazy. We can actually concentrate on something without an onslaught of painful memories. We begin to treasure the memories that we hold in our hearts.

We can laugh again without feeling guilty. We notice that feelings of gratitude bubble up spontaneously without any effort. We find ourselves looking forward to upcoming events with a sense of anticipation, instead of dread.

We realize that we have a deeper understanding of life and of death. We learned something about ourselves, our loved one, and other people during our time of bereavement. We also learned something about God. We understand the old Japanese proverb that says, "Only through suffering and sorrow do we acquire the wisdom not found in books."

We have suffered, but suffering did not destroy us. In some strange way that we may not be able to articulate, suffering made us stronger. Suffering gave us a new outlook on life. The emotional wound that tore us apart when we lost our loved one is starting to heal.

The years that follow will not be as painful as the first. We may not be completely healed, but we are ready to move to a new stage on our journey, with a new level of understanding, new ways to cope, and a new sense of confidence in ourselves and in God.

PRAYER: *Lord, thank you for the gift of your healing love. Continue to shower it down upon me. I am not completely healed, and I still need you. I trust that you will give me everything that I need to go on with my life. Amen.*

❦❦❦❦❦

Robert Browning Hamilton wrote "Along the Road":

> *I walked a mile with Pleasure;*
> *She chatted all the way.*
> *But left me none the wiser*
> *For all she had to say.*
> *I walked a mile with Sorrow*
> *And ne'er a word said she;*
> *But oh, the things*
> *I learned from her*
> *When Sorrow*
> *walked with me!*

❦❦❦❦❦

51. THE NEW NORMAL

In three words I can sum up everything I've
learned about life: it goes on.
— ROBERT FROST

AT SOME POINT in our grief journey, we reach a place where we accept the fact that what we used to call normal is no longer possible. We enter into a new normal. We realize that our lives are different. We still miss our loved one, but we feel as if we are beginning to live again.

It is a process of spiritual and emotional transformation, in which we discover a new sense of meaning and purpose. We develop a new outlook on life. We begin a new way of living. We begin to feel a sense of peace.

As we move into our new sense of normal, we discover new ways of doing things. New people come into our lives. We accept the fact that life will go on — not in the way it had been when our loved one was with us, but in a new way.

We may find that we have a better understanding of ourselves because of the pain we endured. We may become more open, more sensitive, more concerned, and more sympathetic to others. We may feel a strong desire to reach out and help other people who are experiencing the same kind of pain that we experienced.

We may find that our relationship with God has been strengthened. In looking back on our pain, we may see that God was present in our grief. We may recognize that God comforted us in our sorrow. We may see that God carried us when we were unable to take another step. We may realize that God not only heard our agonizing cries but also answered our prayers in ways that we were unable to comprehend at the time.

We reach a new normal when we emerge from the intense pain of grief, and are ready to move into a new stage of our lives.

PRAYER: *Lord, thank you for helping me through my grief. Give me the courage to move on with my life. Strengthen my faith so that I can still invite you to walk with me for the rest of my days. Amen.*

✦✦✦✦✦

One woman realized how much grief had changed her when she looked at old photos of herself before the death of her daughter. She recognized how shallow and superficial her life had been. She had never struggled with deep questions or begged God to help her. Her prior life had been focused on material things and social events. She never had to rely on anyone else. But now it was clear that grief had changed her. Like the grain of wheat that Jesus talks about in the Gospels, her old life had ended, and a new life was now beginning (Jn 12:24).

✦✦✦✦✦

52. IN OUR HEARTS

They whom we love and lose are no longer where they
were before. They are now wherever we are.
— ST. JOHN CHRYSOSTOM

ONE OF THE MOST IMPORTANT parts of the grieving process is to move the memory of our loved ones into our hearts. It takes time, tears, laughter, and patience to accomplish this. But after a while, we begin to understand that even though our loved ones are no longer present on this earth, we have established a permanent place for them deep inside us.

When this happens, memories that used to bring tears and sorrow now bring comfort and peace. We can carry our loved ones with us wherever we go. Nothing can ever take them away from us again.

The great Russian novelist Fyodor Dostoevsky wrote, "It's the great mystery of human life that old grief passes gradually into quiet tender joy."

The joy we experience is not the same as happiness. It is much deeper. It is a profound appreciation for all that this person was, and still is, for us.

We discover that our love continues to grow stronger with each new day. We may still miss them. We may still wish that they were with us in person. But the sharpness of our grief is gone. It is replaced with feelings of tenderness. It is replaced with a new kind of reliance on them. We are no longer dependent upon their physical presence. But we feel them with us always. We begin to incorporate into our lives all of the good things about them. We think about what they would say or do in a certain situation. We find that we can turn to them for inspiration and guidance.

We can rely on our loved ones to pray for us. We can be sure that their love for us has not died. We can believe that when we die, they will be there to welcome us into eternity. We can join the psalmist in thanking God for turning our mourning into dancing, for removing the sackcloth of our grief, and for clothing us with joy (Ps 30:12).

PRAYER: *Lord, thank you for carrying me through my grief. You have transformed my life. You have replaced my pain with a deep sense of peace that the world cannot destroy. For the rest of my days, I will give thanks to you for the love that you have given to me. Amen.*

"*What once seemed such a curse has become a blessing. All the agony that threatened to destroy my life now seems like fertile ground for greater trust, stronger hope, and deeper love.*" — Henri Nouwen

⟵⟵⟵⟵⟵

ACKNOWLEDGMENTS